DIABETIC COOKING FOR SENIORS

KATHLEEN STANLEY
CDE, CN, RD, LD, MSED

American Diabetes Association®

Cure • Care • Commitment℠

Director, Book Publishing, John Fedor; *Book Editor,* Laurie Guffey; *Production Manager,* Peggy M. Rote; *Composition and Page Design*, Circle Graphics; *Cover Design,* Bremmer & Goris Communications, Inc.; *Nutrient Analysis*, Nutritional Computing Consultants, Inc.; *Printer,* Sheridan Books, Inc.

Printed in the United States of America
1 3 5 7 9 10 8 6 4 2

The suggestions and information contained in this publication are generally consistent with the *Clinical Practice Recommendations* and other policies of the American Diabetes Association, but they do not represent the policy or position of the Association or any of their boards or committees. Reasonable steps have been taken to ensure the accuracy of the information presented. However, the American Diabetes Association cannot ensure the safety or efficacy of any product or service described in this publication. Individuals are advised to consult a physician or other appropriate health care professional before undertaking any diet or exercise program or taking any medication referred to in this publication. Professionals must use and apply their own professional judgment, experience, and training and should not rely solely on the information contained in this publication before prescribing any diet, exercise, or medication. The American Diabetes Association—its officers, directors, employees, volunteers, and members—assumes no responsibility or liability for personal or other injury, loss, or damage that may result from the suggestions or information in this publication.

∞ The paper in this publication meets the requirements of the ANSI Standard Z39.48-1992 (permanence of paper).

ADA titles may be purchased for business or promotional use or for special sales. For information, please write to Lee Romano Sequeira, Special Sales & Promotions, at the address below.

American Diabetes Association
1701 North Beauregard Street
Alexandria, VA 22311

Library of Congress Cataloging-in-Publication Data

Stanley, Kathleen, 1963-
    Diabetic cooking for seniors / Kathleen Stanley.
        p. cm.
    Includes index.
    ISBN 1-58040-073-6 (alk. paper)
        1. Diabetes in old age—Diet therapy—Recipes. I. Title.

    RC660.75 .S73 2001
    618.97'64620654—dc21

2001046107

This book is dedicated to my son George,
who came into my life
during the writing of this book
and joined with my heart forever,
and to my wonderful husband Steve,
who is a prize-winning
and much-adored chef in our home.

Contents

A Note about Food Labels

Many food labels in the grocery store use terms that can be confusing. To help you shop and eat better, here is a list of the common terms as defined by the Food and Drug Administration.

Sugar

Sugar Free: Less than 0.5 gram of sugar per serving.

No Added Sugar, Without Added Sugar, No Sugar Added: This does not mean the same as "sugar free." A label bearing these words means that no sugars were added during processing, or that processing does not increase the sugar content above the amount the ingredients naturally contain. Consult the nutrition information panel to see the total amount of sugar in this product.

Reduced Sugar: At least 25% less sugar per serving than the regular product.

Calories

Calorie Free: Fewer than 5 calories per serving.

Low Calorie: 40 calories or less per serving. (If servings are smaller than 30 grams, or smaller than 2 tablespoons, this means 40 calories or less per 50 grams of food.)

Reduced Calorie, Fewer Calories: At least 25% fewer calories per serving than the regular product.

Fat

Fat Free, Nonfat: Less than 0.5 gram of fat per serving.

Low Fat: 3 grams or less of fat per serving. (If servings are smaller than 30 grams, or smaller than 2 tablespoons, this means 3 grams or less of fat per 50 grams of food.)

Reduced Fat, Less Fat: At least 25% less fat per serving than the regular product.

Cholesterol

Cholesterol Free: Less than 2 milligrams of cholesterol, and 2 grams or less of saturated fat per serving.

Low Cholesterol: 0 milligrams or less of cholesterol, and 2 grams or less of saturated fat per serving.

Reduced Cholesterol, Less Cholesterol: At least 25% less cholesterol, and 2 grams or less of saturated fat per serving than the regular product.

Sodium

Sodium Free: Less than 5 milligrams of sodium per serving.

Low Sodium: 40 milligrams or less of sodium per serving.

Very Low Sodium: 5 milligrams or less of sodium per serving.

Reduced Sodium, Less Sodium: At least 25% less sodium per serving than the regular product.

Light or Lite Foods

Foods that are labeled "Light" or "Lite" are usually either lower in fat or lower in calories than the regular product. Some products may also be lower in sodium. Check the nutrition information label on the back of the product to make sure.

Meat and Poultry

Lean: Less than 10 grams of fat, 4.5 grams or less of saturated fat, and less than 95 milligrams of cholesterol per serving and per 100 grams.

Extra Lean: Less than 5 grams of fat, less than 2 grams of saturated fat, and less than 95 milligrams of cholesterol per serving and per 100 grams.

Introduction

How to Use This Book

Congratulations! You've probably been working to manage your diabetes successfully for some time now. You've learned a lot about how to prepare healthy, nutritious meals, get some exercise, manage your medications, and keep your blood sugar levels in range. And now you've picked up this book to find out new ways to eat well as you grow older.

Senior adults with diabetes face new challenges to diabetes care. As we age, our digestive process naturally slows down, sometimes causing uncomfortable symptoms. Our taste buds and appetites may become less strong. Our weight may fluctuate up and down. And cooking may seem like a big chore.

This book will help you stay upbeat and on track as you cope with these changes. The first section offers helpful hints on managing your diabetes meal plan, including how to handle loss of appetite or ability to taste, weight changes, eating out, and possible side effects of your medications. Then find great recipe ideas organized by common nutritional needs of seniors. Want to reduce sodium or cholesterol levels? Try recipes like Cream of Broccoli Soup or Meatballs in Tomato Sauce. Need more calcium or fiber in your meal plan? Make a Berry Frappe or Crunchy Chicken Salad. Food just doesn't taste as good anymore? You'll like Pork Medallions with Orange Sauce.

Changing the way you have cooked for years may seem daunting. The recipes were created using simple ingredients that need minimal preparation. We've intentionally limited how much you need to slice, chop, and dice. We call for inexpensive convenience items such as dehydrated minced onions and garlic powder so you don't have to hassle with peeling and chopping whole garlic cloves and onions. Sliced mushrooms, bell peppers, and other items are also available in grocery store salad bars. The recipes use dried herbs for easy preparation and quick marinade options such as fat-free salad dressings.

After the recipe section, there's an extensive resource list to help you fine-tune your diabetes care plan. You'll find a sample weekly menu and grocery list to show you how to plan ahead for a week of interesting, easy meals. You'll also find out how to plan for emergency days when you may not be able to get to the grocery store for food items. An emergency food shelf is a great way to make sure you'll always be able to make quick, nutritious food for yourself. Finally, a glossary of common nutrition terms provides concise descriptions of nutrition concepts.

Managing Your Meal Plan

You have many great options and methods for eating well with diabetes. If you are newly diagnosed, consult a Registered Dietitian (RD) to learn about your options. Some current methods include the exchange system, food pyramid model, calorie counting, point systems, and carbohydrate counting. Find out what works best for you.

Work carefully with your RD to come up with a specific meal plan that you'll like and stick to. You can include many of your favorite foods, even if you're eating less sodium and fat. You can learn new recipe variations and cooking techniques for your old favorites that will satisfy you just as much. Or visit your RD if you have had diabetes for awhile and are finding it difficult to stay on your plan. You may need to have your meal plan updated or find new recipes or different foods to try.

Eating right is a key factor in your successful diabetes care plan. Together with exercise, medications if needed, blood glucose monitoring, and regular physician visits, a healthy, balanced meal plan will help keep your diabetes in good control and let you live a longer, more enjoyable life.

Handling Meal Plan Changes

If you've just been advised to reduce your sodium, fat, or cholesterol levels or serving sizes, you may feel challenged or frustrated.

Don't worry. Try some of the tips below and you'll be surprised how quickly you can modify your past habits.

Reducing Sodium

- Find out how much sodium you need each day from your physician.
- Read food labels carefully. Focus on the amount of sodium listed on the Nutrition Facts label rather than the ingredient list.
- Replace the salt shaker on your table with a no-sodium seasoning blend.
- In most recipes, you can reduce the amount of added salt by at least half.
- Choose fresh foods as much as possible, rather than processed and packaged ones.
- Use fewer convenience foods—they typically contain lots of sodium to prevent spoilage.
- Avoid cured, pickled, and salted items.
- Look for low-sodium recipes for ideas on breaking the salt habit in cooking.
- Try flavored vinegars on food instead of salt. Save small bottles and refill with vinegars and herbs. Then refrigerate them—most need to be used quickly.
- Experiment with herbs and spices. Try:
  - Allspice (great on meats and baked products)
  - Caraway (use on vegetables and salads)
  - Chervil (use in salad dressings and sauces)
  - Coriander (use on pork, beef, rice dishes, bean dishes, and casseroles)
  - Fennel (use to flavor meat dishes or vinegar blends)
  - Lemon balm (use in beverages, salad dressings, and vinegar blends)
  - Winter savory (try on meats, vegetables, pastas, salads, and vinegars)
  - Tarragon (good with fish, meats, vegetables, salads, and vinegars)

- Wasabi (used to flavor seafood, fish, meats, rice dishes, and vegetables)
- Do not use salt substitutes without consulting a physician beforehand. It is okay to use most sodium-free seasoning blends instead.
- Reduce the amount of salt you use slowly to ease the transition.
- Watch for the health benefits of your salt reduction. These may include improved blood pressure levels, less water retention, and improved heart function. After awhile, you will also be able to taste the natural flavors of foods that were previously masked by too much sodium.

Lowering Fat and Cholesterol

If you have to cut back on fats or cholesterol, you've probably already consulted your health care professional to find out your body's requirements. Find out how much fat is allowed in your meal plan—a healthy diet will still contain some fat. While diet is the primary therapy used to reduce fat levels in the blood, You may also need to exercise or take medications. Have your blood fat and cholesterol levels checked regularly to measure your success. And try the following tips.

- Learn to read labels and identify types of fat (saturated, polyunsaturated, and monounsaturated).
- Compare "light," "low fat," and "reduced fat" items to the regular product. Some are excellent substitutions, while others may be significantly higher in cost, or have other added ingredients such as salt and sugar that make the product less healthy.
- Learn to cook without adding extra fat. Take a cooking class or a supermarket tour for inspiration.
- Have a vegetarian day at least once a week.
- Keep the margarine bowl or butter plate off the table, especially if you have already added fats during the cooking process.
- Replace frying with low-fat cooking techniques such as grilling, broiling, and stir-frying. Use marinades, salsas, and spices for flavor.
- When eating out, ask if dishes can be prepared without fat.

- Talk to your physician and/or pharmacist before using any herbal or food supplement to reduce cholesterol. Chances are if the remedy worked, your physician would have already prescribed it.
- Stay active. Choose aerobic activities when possible.
- Control other heart disease risk factors, including smoking, obesity, and high blood sugar levels.

Reducing Portion Sizes

Since metabolism slows down as you age, your body needs fewer calories every year. Activity levels usually decrease. Portion control is one key to weight management, regardless of which meal planning method you follow. Know what your individual serving sizes should be, and read package labels to find the correct portion size for you. Although it's tempting to buy less expensive large-size food items, choose small-size packages when they are on sale. Or repackage the food into smaller food storage bags or containers to improve your chances of maintaining proper portion control.

When you're just beginning, teach yourself correct portions with measuring cups and spoons. You may also want to measure portions once or twice a month just to prevent portion "creep" from occurring. Try some of the other tips below to stay on track with serving sizes.

- Avoid placing serving bowls on the table (the temptation will be to easily reach for second servings).
- Try eating on smaller plates.
- Use juice glasses (4–5-oz size) rather than tumblers or mugs for juice portions.
- Use the appropriate size glass for the correct portion of milk.
- Try using your hand when away from home to measure portions:
  - Your palm is about the size of a 4-oz piece of meat.
  - Your meat portion should be about as thick as your hand.
  - Your fist size is about 1 cup.

- A handful is about 1/2 cup.
- Your thumb is about 1 tablespoon.
- Eat more slowly and chew foods well.
- Avoid common hazards to portion control:
  - Eating in front of the television.
  - Using large serving dishes.
  - Eating while cooking.
  - Going to all-you-can-eat restaurants.
  - Keeping tempting items that are difficult for you to resist in the house.

Eating Out

Eating out is no longer reserved for special occasions! Most Americans eat out several times each week, so having diabetes should not restrict your ability to eat a nice meal away from home. Follow the suggestions below for a healthy restaurant experience.

How to Order

- Ask plenty of questions!
  - How large are the portions?
  - Is a half-size portion available?
  - Can I substitute _____ for _____?
  - Can the chef bake/broil/grill the meat/vegetable instead of batter frying or deep frying?
  - Can the sauce/topping/dressing/butter/gravy be served on the side?
  - Can the chef cook the dish without adding extra salt?
  - Can the chef make a lighter calorie sauce for the dish?
  - Are light/low-calorie ingredients available (salad dressings, cheese, dairy products, juices, or beverages)?
  - What other options are there for dessert?
- Plan ahead. If you are anticipating a large meal, consider cutting back a bit during the day. But don't get too hungry, or you'll be more likely to overeat.

- Know the menu. Read carefully to learn about your choices. If you like to visit the same restaurants, see if you can get a paper copy of the menu to take to your next nutrition counseling session and ask advice on what to choose.
- Ask that toppings such as cheese, potato sticks, hard-boiled egg, bacon bits, and fried items be left off your salad.
- Ask your physician about alcohol consumption. If allowed, select light beers and wine. Stick with club soda, sugar-free mineral waters, sugar-free tonic waters, and diet sodas for mixers with distilled liquor.
- Prime grade cuts of meat have the highest amount of fat marbled through the meat. Leaner selections may include tenderloin, strip steaks, and filet mignon. If the meat portions are very large, ask your waiter to cut your portion in half before serving it and box the second half to take home.
- If you don't have time to read the menu before ordering, ask for a vegetable plate with or without a small portion of grilled or broiled meat.

Smart Selections

- Choose fresh green salads, broth-based soups, steamed seafood, or baked or grilled vegetable appetizers rather than fried vegetables, cream-based soups, fried seafood items, and potato skins.
- Choose salsas or light salad dressings rather than cheese or creamy dips.
- Choose vegetable toppings and fillings in place of meat toppings for pastas, pizzas, pita sandwiches, fajitas, and calzones.
- Stick to fresh vegetables and fruits at salad bars. Limiting potato and pasta salads, coleslaws with mayonnaise, meats, fried vegetables, shredded cheese, bacon bits, hard-boiled egg, and sweetened fruits.
- Ask for fat-free milk for coffee or tea rather than cream or powdered creamers.
- Use artificial sweeteners rather than sugar or honey. Ask whether the restaurant serves sugar-free or reduced-sugar jams, jellies, and syrups.

- Choose to have either an appetizer or dessert.
- Watch out for condiments! Stick to very low-calorie choices such as black pepper, horseradish, fresh lemon or lime juice, mustard, light soy sauce, flavored vinegar, crushed red pepper, and salsas.
- Limit cheese on sandwiches, burgers, vegetables, and as a topping on the dish. Most restaurant cheese is not low in fat or sodium.
- At steakhouses and roadhouses, bypass the peanut bucket and ask for your salad to be served right away while you wait for your meal.
- Carry sugar-free gum or mints to use after a meal rather than having dessert.
- Consult an expert. There are several excellent books on successfully eating out. Try these, available from the American Diabetes Association:
  - *The ADA Guide to Healthy Restaurant Eating* by Hope Warshaw
  - *The Diabetes Carbohydrate and Fat Gram Guide* by Lea Ann Holzmeister
  - *The Official Pocket Guide to Diabetic Exchanges*

Proper Portions

- If you tend to overeat, do not choose the food bar option. Order from the menu to keep your portion sizes in line and avoid temptation.
- Drink liquids throughout the meal to aid digestion and help slow your eating.
- If portions are large, do not hesitate to ask for a take-home container. Save the food for another delicious meal.
- Order a senior or child portion if you tend to overeat.
- If you are taking diabetes medications, ask your doctor how you can adjust your medication for larger meals. Many medications should not be changed even if meal size alters.
- If you feel you have overeaten, try to include some extra physical activity and water during the rest of the day.

- After you've served yourself in a family-style restaurant, ask that the serving bowls be cleared from the table.
- Have the roll/breadstick basket removed after taking your portion to avoid temptation.
- Split dessert with your dinner partner.

Food and Drug Interactions

Most people are aware that some medications may affect the effectiveness of other medications, or may cause mild side effects. Less well known is the potential impact of some medications on nutrition. Some over-the-counter and prescription drugs have side effects that may impair your appetite, change the way your food tastes, alter digestion, cause dry mouth, affect your sense of smell, and change how your body absorbs or uses nutrients. The impact of the drugs you're taking may be slight or substantial. It is important to ask your pharmacist about all the potential side effects of your medications.

Before a health professional prescribes a new medication, you have the responsibility to inform him or her of your other medication use, your health condition, past medication intolerances, and your typical eating schedule. If you drink alcohol, even occasionally, make sure your physician and pharmacist are aware of this. Alcohol may change the effectiveness of the medication (either increasing or decreasing its effect) or react in negative way with your medication. If you do not follow a standard eating pattern, or follow a different day/night schedule, inform your health care professional. Your morning medication may be intended for people who eat a full breakfast.

If you take medications with or between meals, follow the guidelines as written. Do not change the timing of medication for your convenience or because you want to experiment. The timing of your medication and meals has been carefully considered to produce the greatest therapeutic effect and reduce side effects. This is especially true for diabetes medications

Write out your medication schedule and use a daily pill box to help you stay on track. If you use pill reminder boxes, be aware some medications are not to be taken out of their original container and to be exposed to light and heat. Always read your prescription medication information insert thoroughly to find out about storage requirements. Always discard expired medications.

Set timers to help remind you if you forget to take your medications frequently. Or, plan to take them during typical daily events according to the time of day prescribed, such as right after you wake up, when the mail arrives, or during your favorite television show. If you forget a medication, ask a pharmacist before taking it at a non-prescribed time.

Below is a basic list of some potential food and drug interactions associated with some commonly used medications. This list does not imply your medication will cause a problem, nor does it list every possible side effect that a medication may have. Always check with your pharmacist or physician for more information about any medication you may be taking.

ALTERED TASTE	DRY MOUTH	GASTRIC IRRITATIONS	APPETITE CHANGES	DIGESTIVE DISORDERS
Antibiotics Chemotherapy agents Cold remedies Potassium-based medications	Antidepressants Antidepressants Diuretics (water pills)	Antibiotics Alcohol-containing products Aspirin-containing products	Antidepressants Antipsychotics Sedatives Steroids	Antacids Antianxiety medications Antibiotics Chemotherapy agents Cholesterol-lowering medications Mineral oil-containing products

If you are experiencing unpleasant symptoms that you suspect may be medication side effects, consult your physician as soon as possible. Never discontinue a medication without advice from a physician. Try some of these tips to get the most out of your diabetes medications.

- Use one pharmacy to fill your prescriptions, or at least the same chain. If you use several pharmacies, they may not have complete or up-to-date records to help prevent drug/drug or nutrient/drug interactions.
- Carry a list of your prescribed and over-the-counter medications at all times in case it is needed.
- Share information about alcohol use, herbal supplements, dietary supplements and home remedies with your health care professional.
- If medications are difficult to swallow, ask the pharmacist if the medication is available in a different form—elixirs, liquids, powders, or coated pills.
- If medications cause an unpleasant aftertaste affecting your appetite, follow the medication with a bite of dry food such as toast or a cracker to help neutralize the aftertaste. Ask your pharmacist if it is okay to brush your teeth and rinse your mouth with water after taking the medication.
- Discard any unused prescription medication after your illness has resolved—don't play doctor by trying to reuse old prescriptions.
- Keep a small stock handy of approved over-the-counter medications for mild colds and common health problems. Always have your physician approve of all over-the-counter medications, including pain relievers, cold medications, cough syrups, decongestants, allergy medicines, and antacids.
- Ask if syrups or elixirs can be made without added sugar.
- Find out if medications you take routinely have any affect on nutrient absorption to prevent potential nutrient deficiencies.

Handling Common Problems

It may help to know that you are not alone when you experience some of the less desirable side effects of aging. We all have to cope at some point with increased digestive problems, loss of appetite, diminished ability to chew or taste foods, and stubborn weight changes. There are methods and techniques that will help; read on to find out which will work for you!

Digestive Difficulties

Digestive problems may be the result of food intolerances, poor digestion, or poor absorption. You may have a problem requiring medical treatment. From time to time, most people experience some mild form of digestive difficulty. As people age, their digestive process becomes slower, which may result in occasional uncomfortable symptoms. Some therapeutic daily medications may also cause symptoms to occur more frequently. However, it is important to seek medical attention from a physician for recurring digestive problems such as heartburn, stomach pain, vomiting, constipation, or diarrhea.

People who experience recurring digestive problems will often eat less or limit their food choices. This may lead to undesirable weight loss or lack of proper nutrient intake. Seek medical evaluation before imposing significant changes to your meal plan, and ask your RD for an up-to-date evaluation and new meal plan guidelines. For diagnosed digestive problems that occur infrequently, the following basic guidelines may help.

Gastroesophageal Reflux

- Lose weight if needed
- Watch portion sizes
- Avoid stressful activities just after meals
- Stay upright for at least 1 hour after meals
- Avoid foods high in fat
- Avoid carbonated and alcoholic beverages
- Avoid tight-fitting clothing
- Drink 4–8 oz of water after a meal

Peptic Ulcers

- Avoid alcohol
- Avoid caffeine
- Limit fatty or greasy foods

- Avoid powdered meat tenderizers
- Do not take antacids without first checking with your physician
- Avoid tight-fitting clothing

Mild Diarrhea

- Initially limit intake to liquids and progress to solids as tolerated
- Try applesauce, bananas, plain cereals, breads, and crackers first before adding other solid foods slowly
- Limit high-fiber foods
- Avoid anti-diarrhea medications unless approved by your physician
- Choose lukewarm beverages and foods rather than very hot ones
- Drink fluids, especially water, every hour while awake

Mild Gas

- Limit high gas-forming foods (bran, carrots, dried beans, lima beans, cabbage, peas, onions, cauliflower, and others per personal tolerance)
- Chew food well
- Limit foods high in fat
- Avoid carbonated beverages
- Limit lactose if lactose intolerant, or use lactose-free items

Constipation

- Drink plenty of water and fluids each day
- Stay active
- Avoid sitting for long periods of time
- Increase fiber intake with fresh fruits and vegetables
- Add nuts, dried fruit, and bran granules to salads and other foods
- Try higher-fiber breakfast cereals and whole-grain bread products
- Try prune juice or warm beverages (these old home remedies can often speed relief)

- Avoid laxatives unless you have consulted a physician—try a stool softener instead

Loss of Appetite

True hunger causes physical changes that create discomfort in your body. Appetite is better defined as a desire to eat. There are times when your body may be hungry and need food, but you don't have any appetite. Sometimes the reverse is true. Many factors influence our appetite, such as how we feel emotionally, how we eat, where we eat, available food choices, our ability to taste foods, current health status, lifestyle issues, and our food habits. Before you go any further, get a medical evaluation to find out if you have an underlying medical condition that may be contributing to or be the cause of your change in appetite.

Emotions

Some of us eat best when we are happy, and not as well when we feel sad, stressed, or bored. Others may react to stressful events by turning to food to provide some degree of control or comfort. Food is an important part of our emotional lives. From our early childhood years onward, we usually celebrate special lifetime events and holidays with special foods. Because of this, we generally associate family and social gatherings with food as well. This tie between food and emotions can last a lifetime.

When our health, lifestyle, social, financial, or family situation changes, it can affect our emotional well-being and in turn our appetite. Some common emotional problems such as depression, stress, and boredom can enhance or decrease a person's appetite.

Depression. Depression is the most common emotional disorder in adults and can result in changes of appetite. Chronic emotional stress or distress can contribute to the development of depression.

Having a chronic disease causes physical and mental demands on you. If you feel overwhelmed because of the diagnosis or treatment for diabetes or another health condition, talk to your health care professionals. You may discover resources and support you did not know existed.

If you feel you may be suffering from symptoms of depression, such recurring lack of appetite, lack of energy, feelings of sadness, sleeping problems, concentration problems, or difficulty in controlling your emotions, seek help from a mental health professional. If you are diagnosed with depression, you will find there are many excellent resources and treatment plans to help you.

If emotional problems are affecting your appetite, it will be harder for you to control your diabetes. Poor or irregular food intake increases your risk of hypoglycemia, may result in undesirable weight changes, and may cause a downward spiral in your general health.

Here are some tips to help your appetite when you are coping with depression.

- Consider joining a diabetes support group or a social organization.
- Have regular meal times even if you eat very little.
- On days when you feel well, cook a little extra food and freeze the extra portions for other days when you may not feel as inspired to cook.
- Bring humor to your table—read the comics while you eat or an amusing book.
- Keep easy-to-fix items on hand, so the process of cooking does not further discourage you from eating.
- Try to eat with others as often as possible.

Stress. Everyone lives with a certain amount of daily stress. Stress can help stimulate us to get things done. But if stress occurs too often, is too profound, or is ongoing, it can seriously affect your health.

It is natural to seek comfort of some form or another when you are feeling stressed. Seeking comfort in food, though, will affect the course of your diabetes and make you feel worse in the long run. Try alternative forms of comfort and relaxation when possible before turning to food. Here are some strategies to help.

- Practice stress management activities daily—try relaxation exercises, deep breathing, or journal writing.
- Distract yourself with a new hobby or interest.
- Phone a friend—it is hard to eat and talk at the same time.
- Find other ways to reward yourself after difficult or challenging experiences (rent a favorite video, get your hair styled, or buy a new outfit or gift for a grandchild).
- Drink a full glass of water to fill you up when you feel like eating.
- Keep lots of fresh vegetables available to crunch on if you have to instead of high-fat and –calorie snacks.
- If you feel stress is bothering you so much you can't take proper care of yourself, seek help from a health care professional.

Boredom. From time to time, all of us have been bored. As an older adult, the days of raising a family, going to work, or managing a large household may be things of the past. Living alone, lack of transportation, or limited mobility can significantly impact your ability to enjoy former activities. Too many people watch TV or eat as an antidote to boredom. Try these tips to break those habits.

- Join a volunteer guild, social group, or support group to occupy your time. There are many opportunities for volunteer work that don't even require you to leave home.
- Consider trying new hobbies where you use your hands to keep them busy.
- Follow a regular schedule of waking and sleeping to help keep your appetite on track.
- Sip on water or other zero-calorie beverages through the day rather than eating solid foods.
- Try sugar-free chewing gum.
- Keep sugar-free gelatins and sugar-free Popsicles available for snacks.
- Choose healthy crunchy or chewy items like raw vegetables and fruits rather than creamy or crispy items (think how much harder it is to eat too many carrots than potato chips).
- Chew your food slowly to enjoy the flavor longer.

- Talk to your RD about making your meal plan more flexible if you know you will snack during the day. Together you can develop a meal plan to fit in your food habits.
- Keep food in the kitchen and dining areas only—storing and eating food in other areas, such as in front of the TV, make it easy to overeat.
- Keep temptation foods out of the house. If you must have something, purchase only one portion at a time.

How We Eat

We eat by chewing and swallowing our food, of course. But the natural aging process creates changes in the physical condition of your mouth. Tooth loss, chewing difficulties, and less saliva production are three common physical changes known to affect food intake.

Tooth loss may directly cause self-imposed food restrictions, such as giving up fresh fruits and vegetables, despite still having an appetite for them. Poorly-fitting dentures or partials may make eating painful. Limiting intake to only soft foods may limit your intake of important nutrients and fiber as well. Seek help for tooth loss right away. Have regular dental exams and get properly fitting dentures and partials. Brush and floss each day to keep your teeth in good shape.

Poorly chewed foods may create digestive disorders, which can further impair food intake and appetite. Chew your food well to maximize the amount of time it's in your mouth being exposed to digestive enzymes. Sip on water throughout your meal to keep your mouth moist and make up for less saliva.

If your food choices are still limited, consult a RD to make sure you are getting alternative sources of nutrients. A balanced diet should ideally include foods of many different textures and consistencies.

Where We Eat

Take a look at the place where you eat your meals—is it in the kitchen? The dining room? On the couch? Where you eat can affect how you feel about eating and your appetite as well. Since we must eat several times a day, make sure it's in a pleasant environment!

- Use lots of light (even candlelight) to brighten the area.
- Remove bills, grocery lists, and to do lists from your dining table—looking at them may not help you relax.
- Purchase discount placemats and napkins when they are on sale, then use them throughout the year to brighten the table.
- Try using paper plates with different patterns. Buy them in small quantities so you can change often to create interest. Clean-up is easy too!
- Listen to music to create a more pleasant environment. Try different types of music each night.
- Dine outside when possible, or near a window, and you can watch the happenings of the neighborhood.
- Place favorite photos of family or friends on the table if you dine alone.
- Place different decorations on the table every week—a fresh flower, a seashell from a past vacation, a favorite card from a friend, or a funny comic from the newspaper.

Food Choices

Most people eat the same foods and meals over and over again. These food habits can last so long our interest in eating begins to decline. Even if you are not the most adventurous eater, you can break out of boring food habits with a little effort. Here are some tips to prevent you from getting stuck in a food rut.

- Try one new food item each week.
- Open up a cookbook and find a new recipe using one of your favorite ingredients.
- Eat at a different restaurant every few weeks and examine the food choices and combinations presented. Reading restaurant menus may give you new ideas for your own kitchen.
- Prepare your favorite food item in a different way. For example, instead of plain mashed potatoes, try a twice-baked style or

potato pancakes with chives. Instead of plain grapefruit, try broiled grapefruit or tropical fruit salsa.

- Add one new spice or herb to your usual recipe.
- Go along when a friend grocery shops and see what your friend's favorite foods are.
- Buy small quantities of ten different food items rather than large quantities of two or three things.
- Plan your meals a day or two ahead so you have time to get the necessary ingredients for a new meal.
- When making a new recipe, make extra and freeze individual portions. Then you can eat a wider variety of food without preparing them each time from scratch.

Make Food Appealing

Making food attractive does not have to take a lot of time, artistic ability, or money. Yet it can help stimulate your appetite as well as provide an outlet for creative abilities! Here are some ideas to help you make food more appealing.

- If you use frozen dinners, remove the food items from the reheating plate and place on your own dinnerware before you set it on the table.
- Avoid dinners with food items that are all the same colors. Chicken, mashed potatoes, a piece of white bread, and pear halves would be a very dull-looking meal. Instead, balance lighter colors with darker ones to add interest. For example, chicken with sweet potatoes, whole-wheat bread, and a fresh apple has more eye appeal.
- Add herbs and spices for an easy garnish—try paprika, rosemary, basil, or chives.
- Garnish your plate with a slice of fruit, a couple of fresh red radishes, or green cucumber slices.
- Try a sprinkle of low-fat grated cheese or chopped green onions on salads, potatoes, vegetables, or pasta for a bit of color and taste.

- Serve yourself on your best china from time to time—you deserve it!

Loss of Taste

Three factors work together to give us the remarkable ability to taste and enjoy foods: properly functioning taste buds, a sense of smell, and enough moisture in the mouth. The natural aging process can affect all three of these factors in a negative way, causing changes in your ability to taste food.

Special cells on our tongues allow us to taste. Known as taste buds, these cells have unique chemical receptors to identify sweet, sour, salty, and bitter flavors. As we age, cells detecting sweet and bitter flavors are more adversely affected than those detecting sour and salty flavors. This may be why your cravings for sweet foods can no longer be easily satisfied.

Taste and smell are intertwined due to cells in your nasal cavity as well as the connection between your nasal passages and your mouth and throat. Without your sense of smell, you would quickly discover that taste is as much about what happens before food enters your mouth as it is in your mouth. Have you ever tried to taste food while holding your nose? Or during your last cold, when your nose was stuffy, did you find food less appealing?

The third factor in the ability to taste is moisture, which comes from saliva production within your mouth. Aging reduces saliva production in as many of one-third of senior adults. Other factors may also impair your ability to taste your food, such as smoking, use of other tobacco products, temporary colds and viruses, and some chronic diseases. You cannot reverse physical changes if they have occurred, but you can improve your ability to taste to some degree. To help refresh your taste buds, try these suggestions:

- Do not smoke.
- Do not use smokeless tobacco products.
- See your dentist every six months for mouth, gum, and tooth evaluation.

- Chew foods longer.
- If foods smell unpleasant to you, wait to serve very hot foods until they have cooled down a bit—steam will further enhance strong vapors. Try eating lukewarm or cold items instead.
- If you can't smell as well, serve more hot foods, and let their aroma permeate your nose before eating. Warm items such as breads and liquids to help stimulate your ability to taste.
- If your mouth is dry, sip liquids before and during meals to keep it moist.
- Change the textures on your plate. If foods are all the same texture, it may be more difficult for you to differentiate between flavors.
- Change the sequence of items eaten. Take one bite of this, then switch to a bite of something else, and so on. This practice may help your taste buds stay more stimulated throughout the meal.
- Change seasonings. Add some zest to meals with stronger herbs and hotter spices.
- Make the most out of your ability to detect sour foods—add citrus juices to vegetables, try citrus salsas as a condiment, add a bit of vinegar to vegetables, squeeze lemon into your drinking water, or try tart fruits such as cherries and blackberries.
- Try new recipes to see if spicier food tastes better now.
- Limit bland foods such as white bread, saltine crackers, and plain potatoes. Try herb breads, wheat or seasoned crackers, and a dollop of fat-free sour cream with chives on a baked potato.

Weight Changes

Older adults commonly struggle with weight changes. Many people find weight control to be very difficult. Weight excess (obesity) or weight deficit (being underweight) are challenges at any time of life, but the underlying causes of the problem may be different in an older than an younger adult.

How much should you weigh? Magazine and life insurance weight charts are commonplace tools individuals use to assess whether or not their body weight is acceptable. But a person's acceptable body weight should not be based on just one parameter, such as height or age. Ask your RD, who will assess your body size, body structure and composition, weight history, medical condition, and activity factors, and will also take into consideration your stage of life.

Obesity

The energy needs of the older adult are different from those of a younger adult. The need for calories decreases as we age due to physiological changes in body composition. Lean body mass (muscle mass) decreases as fat mass (adipose tissue) increases. In other words, our body composition changes to a higher portion of fat naturally as we age. Since muscle mass requires more calories (energy) than fat mass, calorie needs are lower as this body transition begins to take place.

Changes in activity will also affect metabolism. Many older adults may be less active than when they were younger due to physical limitations or lifestyle changes. Since less activity means a need for fewer calories (energy), the balance of energy changes. These two factors are common causes of steady weight gain as a person ages, even if caloric intake remains fairly stable.

Obesity may also be caused by overeating. Overeating can be due to lack of knowledge about portion control, increased frequency of snacking, emotional eating, poor meal planning techniques, and poor food choices. Obesity is a risk factor for many health problems such as hypertension, heart disease, poor circulation, arthritis, back problems, and, of course, diabetes. Having diabetes and being overweight increases your risk for diabetes complications as well.

Unfortunately, there is no magic cure or quick fix for being overweight. The cure is to eat fewer calories than is required so the body will use some of its own stored energy (fat). While this cure seems simple, implementing a meal plan for weight control that is satisfying and can be followed for long periods of time is a challenge. Not only will it prevent and control your health problems, but it will increase your energy level and improve your general well-being. Here are some guidelines to consider when you try to lose weight.

- Get a physical exam from your doctor before attempting any weight loss plan. An exam can ensure you are ready for a new eating and exercise program and will also rule out any medical problem that may be contributing to your weight problem.
- Set realistic goals. If you have been heavy all your adult life, it may be unrealistic to think you will finally lose the entire 50 extra pounds you have carried for 30 years. Talk to a RD about your weight loss goals and together you can develop a reasonable plan. Any weight loss will be advantageous to your health!
- Set short-term and long-term goals to help keep you on track. Goals can help keep you focused. Don't forget to reward yourself when you meet any one of your short-term goals. If you don't meet the goal, redefine it and try again.
- Don't be tempted by diets that promise quick weight loss. A meal plan developed with a RD can meet your weight and diabetes management goals. The results may take more time, but they are more likely to last.
- Make sure your weight loss plan includes your favorite foods—if not, chances are you won't be as satisfied with it, and it could become difficult to follow long term.
- Avoid weight loss plans that require you to buy expensive specialty foods. You should be allowed to use foods from your own food pantry and items from a regular grocery store.
- Find support. Losing weight is much easier when you have a person who will provide encouragement and support to cheer you on.
- Do not attempt weight loss during stressful events. After a change in residence, loss of a spouse, or a dramatic change in health, don't try to take on the challenge of weight loss. Wait until a stressful event has eased before trying to lose weight.
- Stay active. Weight loss is more successful when combined with a regular exercise program. If you are just starting on an exer-

cise plan, you may find it increases your appetite just when you are trying to eat less. Keep low-calorie snack ideas (diet gelatins, fresh vegetables, diet Popsicles, and so on) available to help satisfy your appetite.

- Choose a weight loss plan that includes a wide variety of foods to help keep you interested in the plan.
- Decreasing the amount of calories you take in, and increasing your activity level, may increase your risk of hypoglycemia when you have diabetes. Talk to your health care professional about strategies to decrease your risk of hypoglycemia, and always carry hypoglycemia treatment with you.
- Keep a food journal. Write down what you eat and how you feel. Sometimes we find ourselves eating when we are under stress, bored, or sad. Once we identify these trends, this information can be used to help develop a plan to overcome these negative emotions that result in overeating. Use the food diary sample on page 28.
- Leave the table after eating.
- Eat low-calorie snacks before eating out or social occasions where you may be tempted to overeat.
- Take a break halfway through your meal and relax a few minutes. This may help you focus on how full you are getting and slow you down a bit.
- Stay positive. Weight loss takes time!

Being Underweight

Not weighing enough can make you feel tired and weak. It may also increase your risk for developing additional health problems, such as poor immunity against colds, viruses, and infections, as well as many nutritional deficiencies. Weight loss occurs when you eat too few calories for your body's needs. Changes in a person's ability to eat, poor appetite, certain chronic diseases, viral illnesses, poor blood glucose control, and side effects from medical treatments are all possible causes of undesirable weight loss.

If you have experienced unexplained or rapid weight loss (more than one or two pounds in a week), call your doctor for a medical evaluation. You will probably need a strategy from an RD to help you gain weight back at a healthy rate without feeling forced to eat vast quantities of food. To help you gain weight, try the following ideas.

- Stay on a meal schedule to help trigger your appetite response.
- Stock up on your favorite food item—it's not a problem right now if you eat tuna fish three times a day. If it appeals to you, it may help to keep your calorie intake up.
- Keep easy-to-prepare items available.
- Substitute milk and juices for water, tea, and coffee.
- Try six small meals a day rather than three large ones if you feel uncomfortable from eating large meals.
- Consider new recipes to help spark your interest in foods.
- Enlist friends and family to help share cooking responsibilities until you reach your goal.
- Consult a RD about the use of liquid supplemental beverages. These beverages are a great way to get extra nutrition. Since there are many different kinds, check with a nutrition expert to see what works with your meal plan and budget. There are recipes available for homemade supplemental beverages. Common ingredients may include powdered milk, fruit, yogurts, and other products you probably already have.
- Stimulate your interest in food by making it look appealing (see page 21).
- Keep a food diary to help keep track of the amounts of food you are taking in (see page 28). Have a RD do a calorie count to see if you are meeting your calorie goals. It takes 500 extra calories a day to gain about one pound a week!
- Chronic pain can severely affect a person's appetite. If you are suffering from chronic pain, seek medical help to resolve the discomfort.
- Food intolerances may be affecting your intake. If you experience gas, bloating, or other digestive problems frequently, list your symptoms in your food diary to help identify problem foods.

- Do not take herbal supplements or vitamin and mineral supplements without checking with your doctor and your pharmacist. These products may interact with your other medications. Also, some supplements contain higher quantities of nutrients than what the body truly needs. You might be wasting your money.
- Expect weight gain to be a slow process, so stay positive!

Sample Food Diary

Today's Date _____

TIME OF DAY	TYPE OF FOOD	AMOUNT OF FOOD EATEN	BLOOD SUGARS PRE/POST MEALS/ SNACKS	COMMENTS (feelings, environmental factors, signs of food intolerance)
			Pre: Post:	
			Pre: Post:	
			Pre: Post:	

Recipes

Breakfast Ideas

Hot Apple Oatmeal

1 cup quick oats
1 cup unsweetened apple
    juice
1/2 cup unsweetened
    applesauce
1/4 tsp cinnamon

Serves 2

Serving size:
1/2 recipe

1 Mix oats and juice in a small saucepan over medium heat. Bring to a boil, then remove from heat and cover. Let stand 5 minutes.

2 Add applesauce and cinnamon and stir well. For more fiber, add 1 tablespoon dried fruit, nuts, or bran.

Exchanges
2 Starch
1 Fruit

Calories 240
  Calories from Fat . . 22
Total Fat . . . . 2 g
  Saturated Fat. . . . . . 0 g
Cholesterol. . . . . 0 mg
Sodium. . . . . 6 mg
Carbohydrate . . . . . . 49 g
  Dietary Fiber . . . . . . 5 g
  Sugars . . . . 20 g
Protein . . . . 7 g

Cereal Muffins

1 1/2 cups cornflake cereal
1 1/2 cups flour
1/3 cup brown sugar
1 Tbsp baking powder
1/4 tsp salt
1/2 cup unsweetened
    applesauce or baby food
    peaches
1 cup fat-free milk
1 egg
1 Tbsp canola oil

Serves 12

Serving size:
1 muffin

1 Heat oven to 375°F. Prepare 12-muffin tin with nonstick cooking spray (or paper muffin liners). Crush the cereal by placing it in a plastic zippered bag and use a rolling pin or the bottom of a glass to gently crush the flakes.

2 Combine dry ingredients in a medium bowl. Combine liquid ingredients in a separate small bowl. Slowly pour liquid mixture into dry ingredients and stir just until moistened. Pour batter into muffin cups. Bake 20 minutes or until light brown.

3 Makes 12 muffins. Store half in freezer for later use if desired, but wait until muffins have completely cooled prior to freezing. For more fiber, use 1 cup crushed bran flakes cereal.

Exchanges
1 1/2 Starch

Calories 121
    Calories from Fat . . 16
Total Fat . . . . 2 g
    Saturated Fat. . . . . . . 0 g
Cholesterol. . . . . . . 18 mg
Sodium . . . . 195 mg
Carbohydrate . . . . . 23 g
    Dietary Fiber . . . . . . 1 g
    Sugars . . . . 8 g
Protein . . . . 3 g

Sticky Muffins

4 uncooked refrigerator
    biscuits (3/4 oz each)
2 Tbsp reduced-sugar orange
    marmalade

Serves 2

Serving size:
2 muffins

1 Heat oven to 375°F. Spray
4-muffin tin with nonstick cooking spray.

2 In a small bowl, tear biscuit
dough into small pieces. Stir in
orange marmalade until pieces are
slightly coated on all sides.

3 Spoon pieces into muffin cups,
filling 2/3 full. Bake 15 minutes
until puffed and light brown. Add
1 Tbsp raisins or dried cranberries
for more fiber.

Exchanges
1 1/2 Starch

Calories 125
    Calories from Fat . . 13
Total Fat . . . . 1 g
    Saturated Fat . . . . . . 0 g
Cholesterol . . . . 0 mg
Sodium . . . . 371 mg
Carbohydrate . . . . . 26 g
    Dietary Fiber . . . . . . 1 g
    Sugars . . . . 7 g
Protein . . . . 2 g

Breakfast Quesadillas

2 8-inch flour tortillas
1/2 cup egg substitute
Dash black pepper
Dash red pepper
2 slices fresh tomato
1 slice fat-free cheese
1 slice onion (optional)

Serves 2

Serving size:
1/2 quesadilla

1 Heat oven to 375°F. Scramble egg substitute in small skillet.

2 Lay 1 tortilla on a nonstick baking sheet. Spoon cooked egg substitute on top and sprinkle with peppers. Top with tomato, cheese, and onion, if desired.

3 Add second tortilla on top. Press lightly. Bake 5 minutes, flip, and bake 5 more minutes or until cheese is melted. Cut into fourths to serve.

Exchanges
2 Starch
1 Lean Meat

Calories 216
  Calories from Fat . . 33
Total Fat . . . . 4 g
  Saturated Fat . . . . . . 1 g
Cholesterol . . . . 2 mg
Sodium . . . . 451 mg
Carbohydrate . . . . . 30 g
  Dietary Fiber . . . . . . 2 g
  Sugars . . . . 3 g
Protein . . . . 15 g

White Omelet

1/4 cup fat-free cottage
    cheese
1 tsp margarine
3 egg whites
1 Tbsp fat-free milk
1/4 tsp dried thyme
Dash black pepper
1 Tbsp chopped green onion

Serves 1

Serving size:
1 omelet

1 Process cottage cheese in a blender until thick and creamy. Heat margarine in small skillet on medium heat.

2 In a small bowl, whip egg whites, milk, thyme, and black pepper. Pour egg white mixture into hot pan. Swirl mixture around edges of the small skillet. Using a fork, pull the cooked edges inwards so uncooked portion leaks out towards the pan edges. When the top surface is just firm, flip the omelet over.

3 Spoon cottage cheese on 1/2 of the omelet. Top with green onion. Check underside to make sure omelet is cooked, then fold omelet carefully with spatula, or cut omelet in half and add top half to omelet. Remove from heat and serve.

Exchanges
1/2 Carbohydrate
2 Very Lean Meat
1/2 Fat

Calories 132
  Calories from Fat . . 35
Total Fat . . . . 4 g
  Saturated Fat . . . . . . 1 g
Cholesterol . . . . 3 mg
Sodium . . . . 423 mg
Carbohydrate . . . . . . 5 g
  Dietary Fiber . . . . . . 0 g
  Sugars . . . . 3 g
Protein . . . . 18 g

Cinnamon Rice

1/2 cup rice
1 cup water
1 Tbsp fat-free milk
2 Tbsp raisins
1 tsp margarine
1/2 tsp sugar
1/4 tsp cinnamon

Serves 2

Serving size:
1/2 recipe

1 In a small saucepan, bring rice, water, milk, and raisins to a boil, stirring occasionally. Lower heat, cover tightly, and cook 15 minutes on low until liquid is absorbed and rice is tender.

2 Mix sugar and cinnamon together and sprinkle over rice to serve.

Exchanges
2 1/2 Starch
1/2 Fruit

Calories	219
Calories from Fat	20
Total Fat	2 g
Saturated Fat	0 g
Cholesterol	0 mg
Sodium	29 mg
Carbohydrate	45 g
Dietary Fiber	1 g
Sugars	7 g
Protein	4 g

Chocolate Pancakes

1/2 cup flour
1 Tbsp sugar
1 Tbsp cocoa powder
1 1/2 tsp baking powder
1/4 tsp salt
1/4 cup egg substitute
1/2 cup fat-free milk
2 tsp canola oil
1/2 cup fresh berries
    or cut fruit

Serves 2

Serving size:
4 pancakes

1 Heat skillet or griddle on medium heat. Whisk dry ingredients together. Add liquid ingredients and mix until mostly smooth.

2 Spray skillet or griddle with nonstick cooking spray. For each pancake, pour about 3 Tbsp of batter. Cook until edges are firm, flip, and cook other side.

3 Top with fresh berries or fruit to serve.

Exchanges
2 1/2 Starch
1 Fat

Calories 242
  Calories from Fat . . 50
Total Fat . . . . 6 g
  Saturated Fat . . . . . . 0 g
Cholesterol . . . . 1 mg
Sodium . . . . 473 mg
Carbohydrate . . . . . 40 g
  Dietary Fiber . . . . . . 3 g
  Sugars . . . . 12 g
Protein . . . . 9 g

Quick Egg & Hamwich

1 hamburger or hot dog bun
1 hard-boiled egg
1 oz reduced-fat ham slice
1 slice fat-free cheese
    (optional)
1 tsp margarine

Serves 1

Serving size:
1 sandwich

1 Heat oven to 350°F. Peel and slice egg. Place egg slices on bottom half of bun and top with ham and cheese, if desired.

2 Spread margarine on top half of bun. Wrap bun in aluminum foil and bake for 10 minutes or until warmed.

Exchanges
1 1/2 Starch
2 Lean Meat
1 Fat

Calories 263
  Calories from Fat . 108
Total Fat . . . . 12 g
  Saturated Fat . . . . . . 3 g
Cholesterol . . . . . . 227 mg
Sodium . . . . 692 mg
Carbohydrate . . . . . 23 g
  Dietary Fiber . . . . . . 1 g
  Sugars . . . . 5 g
Protein . . . . 14 g

Low-Fat Granola

1 cup oats
1/4 cup wheat germ
1/4 cup slivered or sliced
    almonds
1/4 cup dried fruit
1/4 cup unsweetened fruit
    juice
1 Tbsp honey

Serves 4

Serving size:
1/4 recipe

1 Heat oven to 300°F. Combine all dry ingredients in a bowl. Combine fruit juice and honey in a small cup. Add to dry ingredients and mix well.

2 Spread the mixture on a nonstick baking sheet. Bake 20 minutes, stir, and bake 10 more minutes.

3 Remove from oven and let cool. Store in a container or glass jar with a tight lid.

Exchanges
2 Carbohydrate
1 Fat

Calories 196
  Calories from Fat . . 51
Total Fat . . . . 6 g
  Saturated Fat . . . . . . 0 g
Cholesterol . . . . 0 mg
Sodium . . . . 4 mg
Carbohydrate . . . . . 32 g
  Dietary Fiber . . . . . . 4 g
  Sugars . . . . 13 g
Protein . . . . 7 g

Yummy Breakfast Biscuits

3/4 cup flour
1 1/2 tsp low-sodium baking
    powder
1 tsp sugar
2 Tbsp margarine
4 Tbsp fat-free milk
1/8 tsp salt

Serves 5

Serving size:
1 biscuit

Exchanges
1 Starch
1 Fat

Calories 117
  Calories from Fat . . 43
Total Fat . . . . 5 g
  Saturated Fat . . . . . . 1 g
Cholesterol . . . . 0 mg
Sodium . . . . 168 mg
Carbohydrate . . . . . 16 g
  Dietary Fiber . . . . . . 0 g
  Sugars . . . . 2 g
Protein . . . . 2 g

1 Heat oven to 425°F. In a small bowl, combine flour, baking powder, and sugar.

2 Add margarine, cutting into flour with a fork. Add milk (add a little more if needed) to moisten and shape dough into a small ball.

3 Flatten ball with palm. Fold in half and flatten again. Cut 4 round biscuits, then gather scraps, form into a ball, and cut additional biscuit.

4 Place biscuits on nonstick baking sheet and bake 8–10 minutes or until light brown.

Quick Fixes

Turkey Noodle Soup

1 1/2 cups water
1 10 1/2-oz can vegetable
    soup
1 1/2 cups cooked egg
    noodles
6 oz ground turkey breast,
    cooked and drained
1/4 tsp dried rubbed sage
1/4 tsp dried thyme
Dash black pepper

Serves 2

Serving size:
1/2 recipe

1 Combine all ingredients in a saucepan and heat.

Exchanges
2 1/2 Starch
3 Very Lean Meat
1 Vegetable
1/2 Fat

Calories 358
  Calories from Fat . . 42
Total Fat . . . . 5 g
  Saturated Fat. . . . . . 1 g
Cholesterol . . . . . . 109 mg
Sodium. . . . . 1193 mg
Carbohydrate . . . . . . 42 g
  Dietary Fiber . . . . 3 g
  Sugars . . . . 4 g
Protein . . . . 34 g

Mock Maryland Shrimp Bisque

1 10 3/4-oz can cream of
    potato soup
1/4 cup tomato paste
1 1/2 cup fat-free milk
6 small peeled cooked
    shrimp
Pinch ground red pepper
Pinch ground black pepper
1 tsp dried chives

Serves 2

Serving size:
1/2 recipe

1 Combine all ingredients in a
  saucepan and heat.

Exchanges
2 Carbohydrate
1 Very Lean Meat
1/2 Fat

Calories 229
  Calories from Fat . . 41
Total Fat . . . . 5 g
  Saturated Fat . . . . . . 2 g
Cholesterol . . . . 70 mg
Sodium . . . . 1248 mg
Carbohydrate . . . . . . 32 g
  Dietary Fiber . . . . 3 g
  Sugars . . . . 10 g
Protein . . . . 16 g

Oven Stew

1/2 lb stew meat, cut into
    bite-sized pieces
2 Tbsp flour
1 10 3/4 oz can reduced-fat
    cream of celery soup
1 1/2 cup water
1/2 tsp marjoram
1 tsp thyme
2 tsp Worcestershire sauce
2 tsp dehydrated minced
    onion
1 cup baby carrots
1 large baking potato,
    quartered

Serves 2

Serving size:
1/2 recipe

1 Heat oven to 325°F. Spray a skillet with nonstick cooking spray and place over medium-high heat.

2 Toss the stew meat in the flour to coat, then brown meat in skillet on all sides.

3 Place meat and all other ingredients in a medium baking dish and cover. Bake 30 minutes.

Exchanges
3 Starch
3 Lean Meat
1 Vegetable
1 Fat

Calories 470
  Calories from Fat . 140
Total Fat . . . . 16 g
  Saturated Fat. . . . . . 4 g
Cholesterol. . . . . . . 74 mg
Sodium. . . . . 1259 mg
Carbohydrate . . . . . . 51 g
  Dietary Fiber . . . . . . 6 g
  Sugars . . . . 8 g
Protein . . . . 32 g

Marinated Kabobs

1/2 lb boneless, skinless
  chicken breast,
  cut into chunks
1/4 lb whole white
  mushrooms
1 cup unsweetened
  pineapple chunks
  packed in juice
  (reserve juice)
1/2 medium bell pepper, any
  color, cut into chunks
1/2 cup fat-free Italian
  dressing

Serves 2

Serving size:
1 kabob

1 Stir the pineapple juice and dressing in a bowl, then place all ingredients in bowl and toss. Cover and refrigerate 2 hours. (During this time, if using wooden skewers, soak them in water to keep them from burning.)

2 Prepare broiler or grill. Alternate items on 2 skewers, discarding marinade. Cook 12–15 minutes, turning once, until chicken is done.

Exchanges
3 Lean Meat
1 Vegetable
11/2 Fruit

Calories 284
  Calories from Fat . . 60
Total Fat . . . . 7 g
  Saturated Fat. . . . . . . 2 g
Cholesterol. . . . . . . 75 mg
Sodium. . . . . 386 mg
Carbohydrate . . . . . . 30 g
  Dietary Fiber . . . . 2 g
  Sugars . . . . 24 g
Protein . . . . 27 g

Mediterranean Orange Chicken Salad

1 1/4 cup water
1 5.6-oz box couscous (discard
    seasoning mix)
1/4 cup frozen peas, thawed
1/4 cup frozen pearl onions, thawed
2 tsp extra-virgin olive oil
1/3 cup unsweetened orange juice
1 tsp honey
1 tsp curry
1 11-oz can mandarin oranges, drained
1 Tbsp sunflower seeds
8 oz boneless, skinless cooked
    chicken breast, cut into bite-
    sized pieces and kept warm
1 Tbsp cilantro leaves, torn slightly
    (optional)

Serves 2

Serving size:
1/2 recipe

1 Boil water in a medium saucepan. Add couscous, peas, and onions and stir. Turn off heat and cover pan. Let sit 5 minutes.

2 Combine the oil, juice, honey, and curry in a small bowl.

3 Spoon the couscous evenly on each plate. Top with chicken, oranges, and sunflower seeds. Drizzle dressing over each plate. Top with cilantro, if using.

4 You can substitute cooked brown or white rice for the couscous if you wish.

Exchanges

2 Starch	1 Fruit
3 Very Lean Meat	1 Fat

Calories	365
Calories from Fat.	78
Total Fat	9 g
Saturated Fat.	2 g
Cholesterol	50 mg
Sodium	67 mg
Carbohydrate	47 g
Dietary Fiber	4 g
Sugars.	12 g
Protein	24 g

Snicker Wafers

1 piece white or wheat bread
1 egg white, beaten
1 tsp sugar
3/4 tsp cinnamon

Serves 1

Serving size:
1 wafer

1 Heat oven to 375°F. Cut crusts off bread. Roll bread flat with rolling pin.

2 Brush with beaten egg white on both sides. Combine sugar and cinnamon and sprinkle on one side of bread.

3 Cut into quarters and bake 7 minutes or until crisp.

Exchanges
1 Starch

Calories 83
 Calories from Fat . . . 6
Total Fat . . . . 1 g
 Saturated Fat. . . . . . . 0 g
Cholesterol. . . . . 0 mg
Sodium. . . . . 158 mg
Carbohydrate . . . . . . 14 g
 Dietary Fiber . . . . 0 g
 Sugars . . . . 5 g
Protein . . . . 5 g

Instant Picnic

1 low-fat turkey frank, cut
   into 4 pieces
3–4 small new potatoes
1 single-serving size can of
   yellow corn, undrained
1 Tbsp prepared salsa
1/8 tsp black pepper

Serves 1

Serving size:
1 picnic

1 Heat oven to 350°F.

2 Combine all ingredients in a
small casserole dish and stir.
Cover and bake 25 minutes or until
potatoes are soft.

Exchanges
3 1/2 Starch
1 Lean Meat

Calories 322
   Calories from Fat . . 72
Total Fat . . . . 8 g
   Saturated Fat. . . . . . . 2 g
Cholesterol. . . . . 40 mg
Sodium. . . . . 1282 mg
Carbohydrate . . . . . . 51 g
   Dietary Fiber . . . . 9 g
   Sugars . . . . 17 g
Protein . . . . 13 g

Easy Spinach Soufflés

1/2 cup egg substitute
1 4-oz jar baby food spinach
2 Tbsp flour
1/8 tsp garlic powder
2 tsp grated Parmesan
  cheese

Serves 1

Serving size:
1 recipe

1 Heat oven to 350°F. Whisk all ingredients together in a bowl.

2 Pour into 2 6-oz glass custard cups and bake 20–24 minutes or until puffed and firm.

Exchanges
1 Starch
2 Very Lean Meat
2 Vegetable

Calories 188
  Calories from Fat . . 24
Total Fat . . . . 3 g
  Saturated Fat. . . . . . . 2 g
Cholesterol. . . . . 5 mg
Sodium. . . . . 371 mg
Carbohydrate . . . . . . 22 g
  Dietary Fiber . . . . 2 g
  Sugars . . . . 4 g
Protein . . . . 19 g

Cabbage Patch Casserole

1/2 lb lean ground pork,
    cooked and drained
1/4 cup frozen pearl onions
1 cup cooked rice
2 cups ready-to-use prepared
    coleslaw greens
1 Tbsp cider vinegar
8 oz no-added-salt tomato
    sauce
1/8 tsp black pepper
1/4 tsp caraway seeds

Serves 2

Serving size:
1/2 recipe

1 Heat oven to 350°F. Spoon meat into small nonstick casserole dish and top with onions, then rice, and then cabbage.

2 In a small cup, combine vinegar, tomato sauce, and pepper. Pour liquid over items. Sprinkle with caraway seeds. Cover and bake 30–45 minutes or until cabbage is tender.

Exchanges
11/2 Starch
3 Very Lean Meat
2 Vegetable
1/2 Fat

Calories 289
  Calories from Fat . . 40
Total Fat . . . . 4 g
  Saturated Fat . . . . . . 2 g
Cholesterol . . . . 65 mg
Sodium . . . . 92 mg
Carbohydrate . . . . . . 33 g
  Dietary Fiber . . . . 2 g
  Sugars . . . . 8 g
Protein . . . . 27 g

Swiss Baked Steak

4 oz strip steak or eye of
    round
1 Tbsp flour
2 tsp prepared mustard
1 tsp rosemary
4 small new potatoes
6 small fresh white
    mushrooms
2 Tbsp water
Dash black pepper

Serves 1

Serving size:
1 steak

1 Heat oven to 350°F. Place steak in small casserole dish. Sprinkle flour on top.

2 Spread mustard on steak and add other ingredients to dish. Cover and bake 30 minutes.

Exchanges
3 Starch
3 Very Lean Meat
1/2 Fat

Calories 374
  Calories from Fat . . 64
Total Fat . . . . 7 g
  Saturated Fat. . . . . . . 2 g
Cholesterol. . . . . . . 68 mg
Sodium. . . . . 211 mg
Carbohydrate . . . . . . 45 g
  Dietary Fiber . . . . 5 g
  Sugars . . . . 5 g
Protein . . . . 32 g

Low-Sodium Stuff

Cream of Broccoli Soup

2 Tbsp margarine
2 Tbsp flour
2 cups fat-free milk, divided
Pinch nutmeg
1/2 tsp salt
Dash black pepper
1/2 tsp thyme
1 10-oz pkg frozen chopped
    broccoli, cooked
1 small potato, boiled
1 carrot, boiled

Serves 2

Serving size:
1/2 recipe

1 In a medium saucepan, melt margarine over medium heat. Add flour to make a paste. Slowly add 1 cup milk, stirring mixture rapidly with wire whisk or wooden spoon. Add spices and stir until thickened.

2 In a blender, combine broccoli, potato, carrot, and the remaining milk. Pureé. Carefully pour mixture into saucepan. Stir until well combined. Raise temperature to medium and cook 10–15 minutes, stirring often.

Exchanges
2 1/2 Carbohydrate
2 Fat

Calories 309
  Calories from Fat . 112
Total Fat . . . . 12 g
  Saturated Fat. . . . . . 2 g
Cholesterol. . . . . 4 mg
Sodium. . . . . 322 mg
Carbohydrate . . . . . . 38 g
  Dietary Fiber . . . . 6 g
  Sugars . . . . 16 g
Protein . . . . 14 g

Barbecue Sauce

8 oz no-salt-added tomato
    sauce
1 Tbsp vinegar
2 Tbsp brown sugar
1 tsp dehydrated minced
    onion
1/2 tsp garlic powder
1/4 tsp dry mustard
3/4 tsp chili powder
Dash hot pepper sauce

Serves 10

Serving size:
2 Tbsp

1 Combine all ingredients. Store
in a glass jar in the refrigerator.

Exchanges
Free Food

Calories 17
  Calories from Fat . . . 0
Total Fat . . . . 0 g
  Saturated Fat. . . . . . 0 g
Cholesterol . . . . 0 mg
Sodium . . . . 8 mg
Carbohydrate . . . . . . 4 g
  Dietary Fiber . . . . . . 0 g
  Sugars . . . . 4 g
Protein . . . . 0 g

Easy Baked Potato Bites

2 medium size baking
    potatoes, diced
1/2 red onion, diced
2 Tbsp chopped or torn fresh
    cilantro or parsley
1 Tbsp olive oil
Dash black pepper
1/4 tsp salt

Serves 2

Serving size:
1/2 recipe

1 Heat oven to 375°F. Combine all ingredients in a small bowl.

2 Spread on a nonstick baking sheet and bake 15–20 minutes.

Exchanges
2 1/2 Starch
1/2 Fat

Calories 220
  Calories from Fat . . 57
Total Fat . . . . 6 g
  Saturated Fat. . . . . . . 1 g
Cholesterol. . . . . 0 mg
Sodium. . . . . 11 mg
Carbohydrate . . . . . . 38 g
  Dietary Fiber . . . . 4 g
  Sugars . . . . 5 g
Protein . . . . 4 g

Spicy Pasta Sauce

4 cups fresh ripe tomatoes,
    unpeeled and diced
1 cup water
1/2 cup cooked sliced carrots
2 Tbsp vinegar
2 tsp sugar
2 tsp oregano
2 tsp basil
1 tsp thyme
1 tsp onion powder
1/4 tsp crushed red pepper
1/2 tsp garlic powder

Serves 2

Serving size:
1 cup

1 Cook tomatoes and water over low heat in medium saucepan until tomatoes completely soften, about 30 minutes. Carefully pour mixture into blender.

2 Add other ingredients and blend. Return to saucepan to heat before serving.

Exchanges
1 1/2 Carbohydrate

Calories 111
  Calories from Fat . . 11
Total Fat . . . . 1 g
  Saturated Fat . . . . 0 g
Cholesterol . . . . 0 mg
Sodium . . . . 58 mg
Carbohydrate . . . . . . 26 g
  Dietary Fiber . . . . 5 g
  Sugars . . . . 16 g
Protein . . . . 4 g

Herb Blend for Vegetables

1 tsp dill
1 tsp onion powder
1/2 tsp white pepper

Serves 10

Serving size:
1/4 tsp

1 Mix and shake over salads, tomatoes, squash, peas, zucchini, or carrots.

Exchanges
Free Food

Calories 0
  Calories from Fat . . . 0
Total Fat . . . . 0 g
  Saturated Fat. . . . . . . 0 g
Cholesterol. . . . . 0 mg
Sodium . . . . 0 mg
Carbohydrate . . . . 0 g
  Dietary Fiber . . . . 0 g
  Sugars . . . . 0 g
Protein . . . . 0 g

Oven-Fried Chicken Legs

1 egg white, beaten
2 Tbsp fat-free milk
1/4 cup crushed cornflake
    cereal
1 Tbsp cornmeal
1/4 tsp garlic powder
1/4 tsp white pepper
1/4 tsp black pepper
2 skinless chicken legs
    (drumstick plus thigh)

Serves 2

Serving size:
1 leg

1 Heat oven to 375°F. In a small cup or bowl, combine egg white and milk. Combine cereal, cornmeal, and seasonings in a small zippered plastic bag.

2 Dip chicken legs into egg white and milk, then drop into plastic bag and shake to coat.

3 Bake chicken legs in nonstick baking dish for 25 minutes. Turn and bake an additional 7–10 minutes or until done.

4 For an extra-crispy version, use cracker crumbs instead of cereal. This coating is great on fish, too.

Exchanges
1 Starch
3 Lean Meat

Calories 255
  Calories from Fat . . 75
Total Fat . . . . 8 g
  Saturated Fat. . . . . . 2 g
Cholesterol. . . . . . . 90 mg
Sodium. . . . . 229 mg
Carbohydrate . . . . . 14 g
  Dietary Fiber . . . . . . 1 g
  Sugars . . . . 2 g
Protein . . . . 30 g

Good Fortune Vegetable Fried Rice

2 tsp sesame seed oil
1/2 cup frozen mixed
    vegetables, thawed
1/2 tsp dehydrated minced
    onion
1 cup cooked rice
1 beaten egg white
Dash black pepper
2 tsp lite soy sauce

Serves 2

Serving size:
1/2 recipe

1 Heat oil in skillet or wok over high heat. Add vegetables and onion, stirring constantly. Add rice and heat through.

2 Quickly drizzle egg white over hot mixture while stirring rapidly. Add pepper and soy sauce to serve.

Exchanges
2 Starch
1/2 Fat

Calories 173
  Calories from Fat . . 43
Total Fat . . . . 5 g
  Saturated Fat. . . . . . . 1 g
Cholesterol. . . . . 0 mg
Sodium. . . . . 250 mg
Carbohydrate . . . . . . 27 g
  Dietary Fiber . . . . 1 g
  Sugars . . . . 2 g
Protein . . . . 5 g

Homemade Catsup

6 oz no-salt-added tomato
    paste
1/3 cup cider vinegar
3/4 tsp dry mustard
3/4 tsp onion powder
1/4 tsp paprika
Dash ground red pepper

Serves 16

Serving size:
1 Tbsp

1 Combine all ingredients.

Exchanges
Free Food

Calories	11
Calories from Fat . . .	1
Total Fat	0 g
Saturated Fat	0 g
Cholesterol	0 mg
Sodium	4 mg
Carbohydrate	3 g
Dietary Fiber	0 g
Sugars	1 g
Protein	0 g

Shake on Steak "SOS" Seasoning

2 tsp oregano
1/4 tsp cumin
1 tsp garlic powder
1 1/4 tsp onion powder

Serves 18

Serving size:
1/4 tsp

1 Combine all ingredients.

Exchanges
Free Food

Calories 0
  Calories from Fat . . . 0
Total Fat . . . . 0 g
  Saturated Fat. . . . . . . 0 g
Cholesterol. . . . . 0 mg
Sodium . . . . 0 mg
Carbohydrate . . . . . . 0 g
  Dietary Fiber . . . . 0 g
  Sugars . . . . 0 g
Protein . . . . 0 g

Power Burger

1/2 lb lean ground beef
2 Tbsp oat bran
1/4 cup oats
2 Tbsp fat-free milk
1 tsp dehydrated minced
    onion
Dash black pepper
1/2 tsp canola oil

Serves 2

Serving size:
1 burger

1 Mix all ingredients together except oil and form into 2 patties. Heat oil in skillet and cook burgers until done.

Exchanges
1 Starch
3 Medium-Fat Meat

Calories 296
  Calories from Fat . 153
Total Fat . . . . 17 g
  Saturated Fat. . . . . . 6 g
Cholesterol. . . . . . . 71 mg
Sodium . . . . 73 mg
Carbohydrate . . . . . . 11 g
  Dietary Fiber . . . . 2 g
  Sugars . . . . 1 g
Protein . . . . 23 g

Flavor
Powerhouse

Anytime Fruit Salad

1 cup low-fat (1%) cottage
    cheese
1 11-oz can mandarin
    oranges in juice, drained
1 8-oz can pineapple tidbits
    in juice, drained
1 Tbsp fat-free French
    dressing
2 lettuce leaves

Serves 2

Serving size:
1/2 recipe

1 Combine all ingredients in a small bowl. Spoon onto lettuce leaves.

Exchanges
2 Very Lean Meat
2 Fruit

Calories 171
  Calories from Fat . . 12
Total Fat . . . . 1 g
  Saturated Fat. . . . . . . 0 g
Cholesterol. . . . . 5 mg
Sodium. . . . . 528 mg
Carbohydrate . . . . . . 28 g
  Dietary Fiber . . . . 1 g
  Sugars . . . . 23 g
Protein . . . . 15 g

Cube Steak
with Tomato Sauce

1 tsp dry mustard
1 tsp Worcestershire sauce
1/4 cup tomato sauce
1 Tbsp lemon juice
1/8 tsp black pepper
1/8 tsp ground red pepper
1 1/2 Tbsp extra virgin olive
      oil, divided
2 5-oz cube steaks

Serves 2

Serving size:
1 steak

1 Combine all ingredients except the cube steaks and 2 tsp oil in a small bowl.

2 Heat 2 tsp oil in a skillet over medium heat. Brown the cube steaks on both sides, about 2 minutes each side.

3 Add the sauce to the steaks and cook 3–5 minutes on each side until done.

Exchanges
4 Lean Meat
1 Fat

Calories 264
  Calories from Fat . 141
Total Fat . . . . 16 g
  Saturated Fat. . . . . . . 4 g
Cholesterol. . . . . . . 80 mg
Sodium. . . . . 260 mg
Carbohydrate . . . . 3 g
  Dietary Fiber . . . . 0 g
  Sugars . . . . 2 g
Protein . . . . 27 g

Baked Ham Steak

1 4-oz 95% fat-free ham steak
1 tsp dry mustard
1/2 cup orange juice
1 tsp honey
1/8 tsp cloves

Serves 1

Serving size:
1 steak

1 Combine all ingredients except the ham steak in a small bowl.

2 Place the ham steak in a hot skillet and cover with sauce. Cook 10 minutes at a simmer, uncovered. Turn and cook 5 more minutes or until sauce has thickened.

Exchanges
3 Very Lean Meat
1 1/2 Fruit

Calories 183
  Calories from Fat . . 33
Total Fat . . . . 4 g
  Saturated Fat . . . . 1 g
Cholesterol . . . . 50 mg
Sodium . . . . 1224 mg
Carbohydrate . . . . . . 22 g
  Dietary Fiber . . . . 0 g
  Sugars . . . . 22 g
Protein . . . . 17 g

Shrimp Salad

5 oz cooked, peeled shrimp
1/2 cup mild salsa
1 tsp horseradish
1 Tbsp lemon juice
2 lettuce leaves

Serves 2

Serving size:
1/2 recipe

1 Combine all ingredients and mix well. Spoon onto lettuce leaves.

Exchanges
2 Very Lean Meat
1 Vegetable

Calories 93
  Calories from Fat . . . 9
Total Fat . . . . 1 g
  Saturated Fat. . . . . . . 0 g
Cholesterol . . . . . . 145 mg
Sodium . . . . 345 mg
Carbohydrate . . . . . . 4 g
  Dietary Fiber . . . . 1 g
  Sugars . . . . 2 g
Protein . . . . 16 g

Asian Barbecue Pork Tenderloin

7–8 oz pork tenderloin
2 Tbsp cider vinegar
1/4 cup Homemade Catsup
    (see recipe, page 63)
1 Tbsp brown sugar
1 tsp horseradish
1/4 tsp black pepper
1 tsp onion powder

Serves 2

Serving size:
1/2 recipe

1 Heat oven to 375°F. Place meat on broiler pan.

2 Combine remaining ingredients in small bowl or cup and pour over meat. Bake 20–25 minutes until the meat is no longer pink.

3 Slice tenderloin and spoon sauce over slices to serve.

Exchanges
1 Carbohydrate
4 Very Lean Meat

Calories 185
  Calories from Fat . . 39
Total Fat . . . . 4 g
  Saturated Fat. . . . . . . 1 g
Cholesterol. . . . . . . 65 mg
Sodium. . . . . 65 mg
Carbohydrate . . . . . . 12 g
  Dietary Fiber . . . . 1 g
  Sugars . . . . 8 g
Protein . . . . 24 g

Spring Patties

1/2 lb lean ground lamb or
  veal
4 large or 6 small torn mint
  or tarragon leaves
1/2 tsp onion powder
1/4 tsp black pepper
1/2 cup plain fat-free yogurt
1/2 tsp garlic powder
2 tsp lemon juice

Serves 2

Serving size:
2 patties

1 Mix meat, mint or tarragon leaves, onion powder, and black pepper together and form into 4 small patties. Cook on medium-high heat about 3–4 minutes on each side.

2 In a small bowl or cup, combine the remaining ingredients. Spoon over patties to serve.

Exchanges
3 Medium-Fat Meat
1/2 Fat-Free Milk

Calories 255
  Calories from Fat . 139
Total Fat . . . . 15 g
  Saturated Fat. . . . . . 6 g
Cholesterol. . . . . . . 76 mg
Sodium. . . . . 113 mg
Carbohydrate . . . . . . 5 g
  Dietary Fiber . . . . . . 0 g
  Sugars . . . . 5 g
Protein . . . . 23 g

Chilled Mixed Vegetable Salad

1 cup low-fat cottage cheese
2 Tbsp fat-free French
    dressing
1/4 tsp black pepper
1/2 cup each broccoli,
    carrots, cucumber, and
    tomatoes, cut into bite-
    sized pieces

Serves 2

Serving size:
1/2 recipe

1 Combine the cottage cheese,
French dressing, and pepper in
blender and blend until smooth.

2 Pour over the vegetables and
toss. Chill before serving.

Exchanges
1 Carbohydrate
2 Very Lean Meat

Calories 137
  Calories from Fat . . 13
Total Fat . . . . 1 g
  Saturated Fat. . . . . . . 0 g
Cholesterol. . . . . 5 mg
Sodium. . . . . 626 mg
Carbohydrate . . . . . . 18 g
  Dietary Fiber . . . . 2 g
  Sugars . . . . 12 g
Protein . . . . 16 g

Sloppy Joes

1/2 lb lean ground turkey, cooked and drained
2 Tbsp dehydrated minced onion
1 cup reduced-sodium condensed tomato soup
1 Tbsp vinegar
1 tsp dried mustard
1/4 tsp black pepper
1/4 tsp ground red pepper
Dash hot pepper sauce
2 hamburger buns

Serves 2

Serving size:
1 sandwich

1 Heat all ingredients except buns in a saucepan, then spoon onto buns to serve.

Exchanges
3 Carbohydrate
3 Very Lean Meat

Calories 336
  Calories from Fat . . 39
Total Fat . . . . 4 g
  Saturated Fat. . . . . . . 1 g
Cholesterol. . . . . . . 69 mg
Sodium. . . . . 734 mg
Carbohydrate . . . . . . 42 g
  Dietary Fiber . . . . 3 g
  Sugars . . . . 14 g
Protein . . . . 30 g

Stuffed Steak

3/4 lb flank steak
1 Tbsp prepared mustard
1 tsp olive oil
1/2 tsp thyme
Dash black pepper
1 cup salad croutons

Serves 2

Serving size:
1/2 recipe

1 Heat oven to 325°F. Lay meat on flat platter or board. Spread mustard evenly on meat. Sprinkle with oil, thyme, and black pepper.

2 Spread croutons on top evenly. Roll up lengthwise and fasten with skewer. Place into shallow nonstick baking pan.

3 Bake 40 minutes or until juices run clear when pricked with a fork. Slice to serve.

Exchanges
1 Starch
4 Lean Meat
1/2 Fat

Calories	335
Calories from Fat	141
Total Fat	16 g
Saturated Fat	6 g
Cholesterol	81 mg
Sodium	297 mg
Carbohydrate	11 g
Dietary Fiber	1 g
Sugars	1 g
Protein	35 g

Pork Medallions with Orange Sauce

1/2 lb pork tenderloin
1/4 cup flour
1 Tbsp dry mustard
1/4 tsp white pepper
1 Tbsp dried parsley
2 Tbsp fat-free milk
1 Tbsp olive oil
3 Tbsp sugar-free orange
    marmalade
2 tsp Worcestershire sauce
2 tsp water

Serves 2

Serving size:
1/2 recipe

Exchanges
1 1/2 Carbohydrate
3 Lean Meat

Calories 281
  Calories from Fat . . 93
Total Fat . . . . 10 g
  Saturated Fat . . . . . . 3 g
Cholesterol . . . . 65 mg
Sodium . . . . 137 mg
Carbohydrate . . . . . . 20 g
  Dietary Fiber . . . . 0 g
  Sugars . . . . 9 g
Protein . . . . 26 g

1 Cut tenderloin into 1 inch slices. Combine flour, dry mustard, pepper, and parsley into a plastic zippered bag. Dip pork slices into milk, coating both sides, then put into bag and shake to coat.

2 Heat olive oil in skillet over medium heat. Add meat slices and cook on each side 5–7 minutes until browned. Remove from pan and lower heat.

3 Add orange marmalade, Worcestershire sauce, and water. Stir rapidly with a wooden spoon to prevent scorching. Quickly add pork tenderloin pieces back to pan, turning pieces until coated with sauce.

Low-Calorie Concoctions

Sicilian Vegetables

1/4 cup sliced zucchini
1/4 cup sliced yellow squash
1 Tbsp chopped green onion
1/2 tsp prepared minced
    garlic
2 Tbsp no-salt-added tomato
    juice
1/2 tsp dried basil

Serves 1

Serving size:
1 recipe

1 Heat oven to 350°F. Combine all ingredients in small bowl.

2 Spread on nonstick baking sheet in single layer. Bake 15 minutes, turning vegetables over once halfway through cooking time.

Exchanges
1 Vegetable

Calories 19
  Calories from Fat . . . 1
Total Fat . . . . 0 g
  Saturated Fat . . . . 0 g
Cholesterol . . . . 0 mg
Sodium . . . . 6 mg
Carbohydrate . . . . 4 g
  Dietary Fiber . . . . 1 g
  Sugars . . . . 3 g
Protein . . . . 1 g

Veal Scallopini with Lemon Sauce

4 oz thin veal slices
1 beaten egg white
1 Tbsp flour
1/2 cup dry bread crumbs
1 tsp olive oil
1 tsp margarine
Dash black pepper
2 Tbsp lemon juice
2 Tbsp water
1 Tbsp capers
1 Tbsp chopped green onion

Serves 2

Serving size:
1/2 recipe

1 Dip veal slices into egg white. Mix flour and bread crumbs on small plate. Dredge veal slices in flour and bread crumbs.

2 Heat olive oil and margarine in skillet over medium heat. Add veal and cook 2 minutes. Turn and sprinkle with black pepper.

3 Add lemon juice, capers, and green onion. Cook 2 more minutes.

Exchanges
1 Starch
2 Lean Meat

Calories 197
    Calories from Fat . . 62
Total Fat . . . . 7 g
    Saturated Fat. . . . . . 1 g
Cholesterol. . . . . 51 mg
Sodium. . . . . 333 mg
Carbohydrate . . . . . . 13 g
    Dietary Fiber . . . . . . 1 g
    Sugars . . . . 1 g
Protein . . . . 20 g

Sautéed Mushrooms

1 Tbsp margarine
1 lb washed and stemmed
    mushrooms, sliced or
    quartered
1/4 tsp black pepper
1 tsp dried parsley

Serves 2

Serving size:
1/2 recipe

1 Sauté ingredients together in melted margarine over medium-high heat about 5–7 minutes.

Exchanges
2 Vegetable
1 1/2 Fat

Calories 107
  Calories from Fat . . 60
Total Fat . . . . 7 g
  Saturated Fat. . . . . . . 1 g
Cholesterol. . . . . 0 mg
Sodium. . . . . 75 mg
Carbohydrate . . . . . . 10 g
  Dietary Fiber . . . . 3 g
  Sugars . . . . 3 g
Protein . . . . 5 g

Braised Cabbage

1 cup water
1 reduced-sodium beef
      bouillon cube
1 cup chopped cabbage
1/8 tsp black pepper
1/8 tsp white pepper
1 tsp vinegar

1 Boil water and add all ingredients.

2 Cook uncovered 2 minutes, then cover and cook 5–10 minutes until desired doneness. Drain cabbage to serve.

Exchanges
1 Vegetable

Calories 22
   Calories from Fat . . . 2
Total Fat . . . . 0 g
   Saturated Fat. . . . . . . 0 g
Cholesterol. . . . . 0 mg
Sodium. . . . . 268 mg
Carbohydrate . . . . 5 g
   Dietary Fiber . . . . 2 g
   Sugars . . . . 3 g
Protein . . . . 1 g

Dilly Cucumber

1 small cucumber, peeled
    and sliced
1 Tbsp chopped green onion
1 tsp chopped pimiento
2 Tbsp fat-free Italian
    dressing
1/2 tsp dried dill

Serves 1

Serving size:
1 recipe

1 Combine all ingredients and chill at least 2 hours.

Exchanges
1 Vegetable

Calories 32
  Calories from Fat . . . 1
Total Fat . . . . 0 g
  Saturated Fat. . . . . . . 0 g
Cholesterol. . . . . 0 mg
Sodium . . . . 314 mg
Carbohydrate . . . . 7 g
  Dietary Fiber . . . . 1 g
  Sugars . . . . 5 g
Protein . . . . 1 g

Baked Onion

1 medium vidalia or other
    sweet onion, peeled and
    quartered
2 Tbsp tomato paste
1/2 tsp Italian seasoning

Serves 1

Serving size:
1 recipe

1 Heat oven to 350°F. Brush onion with tomato paste and sprinkle with seasoning.

2 Wrap in aluminum foil, leaving an airspace, and bake 1 hour or until tender.

Exchanges
1 Starch

Calories 86
  Calories from Fat . . . 5
Total Fat . . . . 1 g
  Saturated Fat. . . . . . . 0 g
Cholesterol. . . . . 0 mg
Sodium. . . . . 26 mg
Carbohydrate . . . . . . 19 g
  Dietary Fiber . . . . 4 g
  Sugars . . . . 10 g
Protein . . . . 3 g

Pepper Parade

1/4 green bell pepper,
    cut into strips
1/4 red bell pepper,
    cut into strips
1/4 yellow bell pepper,
    cut into strips
1 tsp olive oil
2 Tbsp pineapple juice
    (or lemon juice)
2 tsp lite soy sauce

Serves 1

Serving size:
1 recipe

1 Sauté peppers in oil over medium-high heat until slightly soft, about 5 minutes.

2 Add juice and soy sauce, heat through, and serve.

Exchanges
2 Vegetable
1 Fat

Calories 86
  Calories from Fat . . 39
Total Fat . . . . 4 g
  Saturated Fat. . . . . . 1 g
Cholesterol. . . . . 0 mg
Sodium. . . . . 406 mg
Carbohydrate . . . . . 12 g
  Dietary Fiber . . . . . . 2 g
  Sugars . . . . 7 g
Protein . . . . 1 g

Coleslaw Salad

1 .3-oz pkg sugar-free lemon
   or lime gelatin
1 1/2 cups ready-to-use
   shredded coleslaw
1 Tbsp fat-free nondairy
   whipped topping

Serves 4

Serving size:
1/4 recipe

1 Prepare gelatin as directed, stirring in coleslaw.

2 Pour into desired mold and chill until set, about 4 hours. Top with whipped topping.

Exchanges
Free Food

Calories 16
  Calories from Fat . . . 0
Total Fat . . . . 0 g
  Saturated Fat. . . . . . . 0 g
Cholesterol. . . . . 0 mg
Sodium . . . . 63 mg
Carbohydrate . . . . 2 g
  Dietary Fiber . . . . 0 g
  Sugars . . . . 1 g
Protein . . . . 2 g

Zucchini Burgers

1 Tbsp plus 1 tsp olive oil
2 Tbsp chopped green onion
1 cup finely grated zucchini
1/2 cup dry bread crumbs or
        cracker crumbs
2 beaten egg whites
2 Tbsp flour
1 tsp dried basil
1 Tbsp flour

Serves 2

Serving size:
1 burger

1 Heat 1 Tbsp oil in skillet over medium heat. Add onions and cook until soft.

2 Combine onions and remaining ingredients except 1 Tbsp flour in a bowl. Make 2 patties and dredge in flour.

3 Cook patties in skillet over medium heat about 5 minutes on each side.

Exchanges
2 Starch
2 Fat

Calories 239
    Calories from Fat . . 88
Total Fat . . . . 10 g
    Saturated Fat. . . . . . . 2 g
Cholesterol. . . . . 0 mg
Sodium. . . . . 292 mg
Carbohydrate . . . . . . 29 g
    Dietary Fiber . . . . 2 g
    Sugars . . . . 3 g
Protein . . . . 9 g

Tangy Green Beans

1 8-oz can green beans,
    drained
1/4 cup water
1 Tbsp prepared spicy brown
    mustard
1/4 tsp black pepper

Serves 2

Serving size:
1/2 cup

1 Combine all ingredients
and heat.

Exchanges
1 Vegetable

Calories 21
  Calories from Fat . . . 4
Total Fat . . . . 0 g
  Saturated Fat. . . . . . . 0 g
Cholesterol. . . . . 0 mg
Sodium. . . . . 352 mg
Carbohydrate . . . . 4 g
  Dietary Fiber . . . . 1 g
  Sugars . . . . 2 g
Protein . . . . 2 g

Fiber-Rich Foods

Spiced Pear Salad

1 large pear, seeded, cut into
    chunks
2 tsp lemon juice
1 Tbsp raisins
1 Tbsp plus 1 tsp fat-free
    mayonnaise
1/4 tsp pumpkin pie spice
Crisp lettuce leaves

Serves 1

Serving size:
1 recipe

1 Mix all ingredients except lettuce. Spoon on top of lettuce
leaves to serve.

Exchanges
3 Fruit

Calories 170
  Calories from Fat . . . 8
Total Fat . . . . 1 g
  Saturated Fat. . . . . . . 0 g
Cholesterol. . . . . 0 mg
Sodium. . . . . 144 mg
Carbohydrate . . . . . . 43 g
  Dietary Fiber . . . . 6 g
  Sugars . . . . 33 g
Protein . . . . 2 g

Fiesta Salad

1 11-oz can Mexican-style
    corn, drained
1/4 cup rinsed and drained
    kidney or black beans
1 tsp dehydrated minced
    onion
1/4 cup prepared salsa
1 slice reduced-fat American
    cheese, torn into small
    pieces
2 lettuce leaves
6 cherry tomatoes, halved

Serves 2

Serving size:
1/2 recipe

1 Combine corn, beans, onion, salsa, and cheese in a small bowl. Spoon mixture onto lettuce leaves and top with cherry tomatoes.

Exchanges
1 Starch
1 Vegetable
1/2 Fat

Calories 132
  Calories from Fat . . 23
Total Fat . . . . 3 g
  Saturated Fat. . . . . . . 1 g
Cholesterol. . . . . 5 mg
Sodium. . . . . 422 mg
Carbohydrate . . . . . . 24 g
  Dietary Fiber . . . . 4 g
  Sugars . . . . 6 g
Protein . . . . 7 g

Bayou Lima Beans

1 cup cooked lima beans
2 Tbsp prepared salsa
1/2 tsp dried parsley
2 tsp imitation bacon bits
1 tsp Worcestershire sauce

Serves 2

Serving size:
1/2 recipe

1 Combine all ingredients and stir well.

Exchanges
1 Starch

Calories	89
Calories from Fat	. . . 6
Total Fat	1 g
Saturated Fat.	0 g
Cholesterol.	0 mg
Sodium.	140 mg
Carbohydrate	16 g
Dietary Fiber	5 g
Sugars	3 g
Protein	6 g

Arizona Pie

1/2 lb lean ground beef
1 Tbsp dehydrated minced
    onion
1 tsp garlic powder
1 15-oz can pinto beans,
    rinsed and drained
6 oz no-added-salt tomato
    juice
1/4 cup prepared salsa
1 cup reduced-fat baking mix
1/2 cup cornmeal
1/2 cup fat-free milk
1 oz baked tortilla chips

Serves 4

Serving size:
1/4 pie

1 Heat oven to 400°F. Cook beef and drain. Add onion, garlic, beans, tomato juice, and salsa to pan. Heat for 5 minutes on medium heat, stirring well.

2 In a small bowl, combine baking mix, cornmeal, and milk.

3 Spoon meat mixture into non-stick pie pan. Drop dough mixture by tablespoonfuls in center of pie. Bake 20 minutes or until dough mixture is puffed and lightly brown.

4 Remove from oven. Place tortilla chips around outer edge of pie to imitate a crust.

Exchanges
4 Starch
1 Fat
1 Lean Meat

Calories 413
  Calories from Fat . 109
Total Fat . . . . 12 g
  Saturated Fat. . . . . . . 4 g
Cholesterol. . . . . 36 mg
Sodium. . . . . 657 mg
Carbohydrate . . . . . . 56 g
  Dietary Fiber . . . . 9 g
  Sugars . . . . 9 g
Protein . . . . 22 g

Light Greens

8 oz fresh mixed greens
(mustard, turnip, or
collard)
2 cups water
1 reduced-sodium beef
bouillon cube
2 tsp dehydrated minced
onion
1 tsp vinegar

Serves 2

Serving size:
1/2 recipe

1 Wash, trim, and chop greens.
Bring 2 cups water, bouillon,
and onion to a boil.

2 Add greens and cook just until
tender, 9–12 minutes. Remove
from heat, drain, and add vinegar.

Exchanges
2 Vegetable

Calories 42
  Calories from Fat . . . 5
Total Fat . . . . 1 g
  Saturated Fat. . . . . . . 0 g
Cholesterol. . . . . 0 mg
Sodium. . . . . 216 mg
Carbohydrate . . . . . . 8 g
  Dietary Fiber . . . . 4 g
  Sugars . . . . 1 g
Protein . . . . 3 g

Smothered Baked Portabello Mushroom

1 large cap portabello
    mushroom
2 Tbsp low-fat ricotta cheese
1/4 tsp garlic powder
1/4 black pepper
1 cup cooked pasta (linguini,
    spaghetti, or fettuccini)
1/2 cup prepared pasta sauce
1/4 cup shredded low-fat
    mozzarella cheese

Serves 1

Serving size:
1 recipe

1 Heat oven to 350°F. Stem mushroom and sauté in nonstick pan 2–3 minutes on each side.

2 Spoon ricotta cheese into mushroom cavity and sprinkle with garlic powder and pepper.

3 Place pasta in a shallow nonstick baking dish. Pour 1/2 cup sauce over pasta. Place mushroom cap side up on top of pasta.

4 Pour remaining sauce over mushroom and sprinkle with cheese. Bake 20 minutes or until cheese bubbles.

Exchanges
4 Starch
1 Lean Meat
2 Vegetable

Calories 413
  Calories from Fat . . 71
Total Fat . . . . 8 g
  Saturated Fat. . . . . . . 4 g
Cholesterol. . . . . . . 28 mg
Sodium. . . . . 232 mg
Carbohydrate . . . . . . 71 g
  Dietary Fiber . . . . 8 g
  Sugars . . . . 17 g
Protein . . . . 23 g

Crunchy Chicken Salad

3 oz cooked skinless chicken breast, cut into bite-sized pieces
1/4 cup sliced water chestnuts
1/4 red pepper, cut into bite-sized pieces
1 1/2 cups lettuce leaves
1/4 cup chow mein noodles
1 tsp lite soy sauce
1 Tbsp lemon juice
2 tsp sesame seed oil or canola oil
1 tsp sesame seeds

Serves 1

Serving size:
1 recipe

1 In a salad bowl, combine chicken, water chestnuts, pepper, lettuce, and noodles.

2 In a small cup, mix the remaining ingredients and pour on top of salad.

Exchanges
1/2 Starch
3 Lean Meat
2 Vegetable
2 Fat

Calories 345
  Calories from Fat . 155
Total Fat . . . . 17 g
  Saturated Fat. . . . . . . 4 g
Cholesterol. . . . . . . 72 mg
Sodium. . . . . 328 mg
Carbohydrate . . . . . . 19 g
  Dietary Fiber . . . . 4 g
  Sugars . . . . 5 g
Protein . . . . 30 g

Perfect Pot Roast

1/2 lb pot roast
1 tsp prepared minced garlic
1/8 tsp black pepper
1 tsp thyme
1 tsp oregano
2 small baking potatoes, cut
    into quarters
1 small red onion, peeled
    and cut into quarters
1/2 cup baby carrots
1 cup fat-free chicken broth

Serves 2

Serving size:
1/2 recipe

1 Heat oven to 350°F. Place meat in baking dish and sprinkle with garlic and herbs.

2 Add vegetables and pour broth in bottom of dish. Cover and bake 1 hour or until done.

Exchanges
1 1/2 Starch
3 Lean Meat
2 Vegetable

Calories 321
  Calories from Fat . . 60
Total Fat . . . . 7 g
  Saturated Fat. . . . . . 2 g
Cholesterol. . . . . . . 68 mg
Sodium. . . . . 329 mg
Carbohydrate . . . . . 34 g
  Dietary Fiber . . . . . . 4 g
  Sugars . . . . 9 g
Protein . . . . 30 g

Chicken Casserole

1 Tbsp margarine, divided
6 oz skinless chicken breast,
    cut into bite-sized pieces
1/4 lb chopped fresh
    mushrooms
1 Tbsp flour
1 cup fat-free milk
1 tsp onion powder
1/2 tsp white pepper
1/2 tsp thyme
1 1/2 cup cooked brown rice
1/2 cup frozen green peas
1 Tbsp golden raisins
1 Tbsp chopped parsley

Serves 2

Serving size:
1/2 recipe

1 Melt 1/2 Tbsp margarine over medium heat in large skillet. Add chicken and mushrooms and brown on all sides. Remove from skillet.

2 Melt remaining 1/2 Tbsp margarine in skillet. Sprinkle flour into skillet and slowly add milk, stirring constantly. Stir until slightly thickened.

3 Stir in onion powder, pepper, thyme, rice, peas, raisins, and chicken mixture. Cook 10 minutes. Sprinkle with parsley to serve.

Exchanges
3 1/2 Starch
3 Lean Meat

Calories 430
  Calories from Fat . . 88
Total Fat . . . . 10 g
  Saturated Fat . . . . . . 2 g
Cholesterol . . . . 54 mg
Sodium . . . . 220 mg
Carbohydrate . . . . . . 54 g
  Dietary Fiber . . . . 6 g
  Sugars . . . . 12 g
Protein . . . . 31 g

Layered Pasta Casserole

1/2 lb lean ground turkey
1 tsp oregano
1/2 tsp garlic powder
1/2 tsp black pepper
1/8 tsp ground red pepper
2 1/2 cups cooked elbow
    macaroni
2 tsp olive oil
1 8-oz can no-added-salt
    tomato sauce
1 beaten egg white
2 cups fresh spinach leaves,
    blanched until wilted

Serves 2

Serving size:
1/2 recipe

1 Heat oven to 350°F. Cook turkey in nonstick skillet until done. Mix in seasonings and set mixture aside.

2 Combine pasta, egg white, olive oil, and tomato sauce in a bowl. Spoon half of this mixture into a nonstick loaf pan.

3 Spoon the meat over the pasta, spreading evenly. Put the spinach leaves on top of the meat, then pour the remaining pasta over the spinach.

4 Flatten with a spatula to help bind ingredients. Bake 15–20 minutes.

Exchanges
3 1/2 Starch
3 Very Lean Meat
1 Vegetable
1 Fat

Calories 464
  Calories from Fat . . 84
Total Fat . . . . 9 g
  Saturated Fat. . . . . . . 1 g
Cholesterol. . . . . 62 mg
Sodium. . . . . 138 mg
Carbohydrate . . . . . . 56 g
  Dietary Fiber . . . . 4 g
  Sugars . . . . 8 g
Protein . . . . 35 g

Super Snacks

Apple or Pear Dip

8 oz fat-free cream cheese, softened
1 tsp vanilla
2 Tbsp reduced-calorie maple-flavored pancake syrup

Serves 4

Serving size:
1/4 recipe

1 Mix ingredients with a fork and serve with sliced apple or pear.

2 Store remaining dip in refrigerator in a sealed container.

Exchanges
1/2 Carbohydrate
1 Very Lean Meat

Calories 60
  Calories from Fat . . . 0
Total Fat . . . . 0 g
  Saturated Fat. . . . . . . 0 g
Cholesterol. . . . . 7 mg
Sodium. . . . . 333 mg
Carbohydrate . . . . 6 g
  Dietary Fiber . . . . 0 g
  Sugars . . . . 4 g
Protein . . . . 8 g

Cranberry Spread

2 oz whole cranberry sauce
8 oz fat-free cream cheese,
   softened

Serves 4

Serving size:
1/4 recipe

1 Mix ingredients with a fork and serve with toasted bread or Melba toast.

2 Store remaining spread in refrigerator in a sealed container.

Exchanges
1/2 Carbohydrate
1 Very Lean Meat

Calories 72
  Calories from Fat . . . 0
Total Fat . . . . 0 g
  Saturated Fat. . . . . . . 0 g
Cholesterol. . . . . 7 mg
Sodium . . . . 306 mg
Carbohydrate . . . . 9 g
  Dietary Fiber . . . . 0 g
  Sugars . . . . 7 g
Protein . . . . 8 g

Nacho Cheese Dip

2 slices fat-free cheese, torn
     into small pieces
1/4 cup prepared salsa
Dash hot pepper sauce

Serves 2

Serving size:
1/2 recipe

1 Heat salsa and cheese bits until cheese is melted. Add hot sauce and stir.

2 Serve with baked tortilla chips or toasted wheat tortillas.

Exchanges
1 Very Lean Meat

Calories 35
   Calories from Fat . . . 0
Total Fat . . . . 0 g
   Saturated Fat . . . . 0 g
Cholesterol . . . . 0 mg
Sodium . . . . 372 mg
Carbohydrate . . . . . . 4 g
   Dietary Fiber . . . . 0 g
   Sugars . . . . 3 g
Protein . . . . 5 g

Toast and Jam Treat

1/4 cup low-fat cottage
    cheese
2 Tbsp low-sugar jam
1 Tbsp fat-free dry milk
    powder
1 slice toast

Serves 1

Serving size:
1 piece

1 In a blender or food processor, combine cottage cheese, jam, and dry milk powder and spread on toast.

Exchanges
1 Starch
1 Very Lean Meat
1 Fruit

Calories 168
  Calories from Fat . . 14
Total Fat . . . . 2 g
  Saturated Fat. . . . . . . 0 g
Cholesterol. . . . . 3 mg
Sodium. . . . . 389 mg
Carbohydrate . . . . . . 28 g
  Dietary Fiber . . . . 1 g
  Sugars . . . . 10 g
Protein . . . . 10 g

Graham Cracker Parfait

2 squares low-fat graham
    crackers
1/4 cup fat-free nondairy
    whipped topping
1 cup fresh fruit, cut into
    bite-sized pieces

Serves 1

Serving size:
1 recipe

1 Crumble 1 cracker square into
bottom of a large wine glass or
coffee mug.

2 Top with 1/2 cup fruit, then half
of whipped topping, then fruit,
and then topping.

3 Crumble remaining graham
cracker on top to serve.

Exchanges
2 1/2 Carbohydrate

Calories 153
    Calories from Fat . . . 7
Total Fat . . . . 1 g
    Saturated Fat . . . . . . 0 g
Cholesterol . . . . 0 mg
Sodium . . . . 64 mg
Carbohydrate . . . . . . 36 g
    Dietary Fiber . . . . 3 g
    Sugars . . . . 25 g
Protein . . . . 2 g

Garlic Cheese Bites

5 3/4-oz refrigerator biscuits
2 oz part-skim string cheese
    (2 mozzarella sticks)
1/8 tsp garlic powder

Serves 1

Serving size:
1 cheese bite

1 Heat oven to 400°F. With palm of hand, flatten each biscuit on cutting board. Cut a 2-inch piece of cheese.

2 Place cheese piece in center of biscuit and roll up to seal edges tightly. Sprinkle each biscuit with garlic powder.

3 Place biscuits on nonstick baking sheet and bake 10–12 minutes or until light brown.

Exchanges
1/2 Starch
1/2 Fat

Calories 79
  Calories from Fat . . 22
Total Fat . . . . 2 g
  Saturated Fat. . . . . . 1 g
Cholesterol. . . . . 6 mg
Sodium . . . . 233 mg
Carbohydrate . . . . . . 10 g
  Dietary Fiber . . . . 0 g
  Sugars . . . . 1 g
Protein . . . . 4 g

Zucchini Snacks

1/4 cup fat-free cottage cheese

1/2 tsp dehydrated minced onion

1/2 tsp dill

1 small zucchini (6–8 inches), cut lengthwise

1 Blend cottage cheese with dill and onion with fork until thoroughly combined. Scoop out small amount of inside of zucchini along its length.

2 Spread cheese mixture inside of zucchini, top with other half, and set in refrigerator for 1 hour to firm. Cut into 1-inch slices to serve.

Exchanges
1 Very Lean Meat
1 Vegetable

Calories 56
  Calories from Fat . . . 2
Total Fat . . . . 0 g
  Saturated Fat. . . . . . . 0 g
Cholesterol . . . . 3 mg
Sodium . . . . 208 mg
Carbohydrate . . . . . . 6 g
  Dietary Fiber . . . . 1 g
  Sugars . . . . 3 g
Protein . . . . 8 g

Show Time Mix

6 cups air-popped popcorn
1/2 cup dry roasted soynuts
    (or peanuts)
2 cups Corn Chex(tm) cereal
1 oz pretzel sticks
1 tsp Old Bay seasoning
1 tsp onion powder

Serves 6

Serving size:
1/6 recipe

1 Mix popcorn, nuts, cereal, and pretzels in a large bowl. Spray lightly with nonstick cooking spray and sprinkle with seasoning and onion powder.

2 Store in covered container. For a spicier variation, add 1 1/2 tsp chili powder.

Exchanges
1 1/2 Starch
1/2 Fat

Calories 147
  Calories from Fat . . 23
Total Fat . . . . 3 g
  Saturated Fat . . . . 0 g
Cholesterol . . . . 0 mg
Sodium . . . . 358 mg
Carbohydrate . . . . . . 23 g
  Dietary Fiber . . . . 4 g
  Sugars . . . . 2 g
Protein . . . . 8 g

Hot Skins

1 medium baked potato
1/4 tsp oregano
1/8 tsp garlic powder
1/8 tsp black pepper
1/8 tsp paprika

1 Heat oven to 400°F. Cut cooled baked potato in half crosswise.

2 Scoop out insides and reserve for another use, leaving a thin layer of potato along the skin. Cut in half again lengthwise and place on baking sheet.

3 Spray with nonstick cooking spray. Sprinkle with seasonings and bake 10 minutes or until crisp.

4 Dip skins in mustard, salsa, homemade catsup, or non-fat sour cream.

Exchanges
1 1/2 Starch

Calories 97
  Calories from Fat . . . 1
Total Fat . . . . 0 g
  Saturated Fat . . . . 0 g
Cholesterol . . . . 0 mg
Sodium . . . . 10 mg
Carbohydrate . . . . . . 23 g
  Dietary Fiber . . . . 4 g
  Sugars . . . . 1 g
Protein . . . . 2 g

Blue Cheese Vegetable Roll-Up

1 whole wheat or corn
   tortilla
1 Tbsp low-fat blue cheese
   dressing
2 4-inch celery sticks
2 4-inch carrot sticks

Serves 1

Serving size:
1 recipe

1 Heat tortilla per package directions.

2 Spread dressing on tortilla, add celery and carrot sticks to one end of tortilla, and roll up.

Exchanges
2 Starch
1 Vegetable
1 Fat

Calories 234
   Calories from Fat . . 65
Total Fat . . . . 7 g
   Saturated Fat. . . . . . 2 g
Cholesterol. . . . . 1 mg
Sodium. . . . . 442 mg
Carbohydrate . . . . . 36 g
   Dietary Fiber . . . . . . 3 g
   Sugars . . . . 3 g
Protein . . . . 6 g

Low or No Cholesterol

Meatballs in Tomato Sauce

1/2 lb lean ground beef
1 cup cooked brown or white
    rice
1 egg white
1 tsp dehydrated minced
    onion
1 tsp oregano
Dash black pepper
1 cup reduced-sodium
    condensed tomato soup
1/2 cup water

Serves 2

Serving size:
1/2 recipe

1 Combine beef, rice, egg white, onion, oregano, and pepper in small bowl. Shape into balls.

2 Brown meatballs in nonstick medium skillet on all sides. Whisk in tomato soup and water and bring to a boil. Cover, reduce heat, and cook for 20 minutes.

Exchanges
2 1/2 Starch
3 Medium-Fat Meat

Calories 442
  Calories from Fat . 155
Total Fat . . . . 17 g
  Saturated Fat. . . . . . . 6 g
Cholesterol. . . . . 71 mg
Sodium. . . . . 598 mg
Carbohydrate . . . . . . 41 g
  Dietary Fiber . . . . 3 g
  Sugars . . . . 11 g
Protein . . . . 29 g

Asian Tuna Casserole

1 6-oz can water-packed
    tuna
1 cup cooked white rice or
    noodles
1/4 cup water chestnuts
1 tsp dehydrated minced
    onion
1/2 cup frozen green peas,
    thawed
1/4 cup cashew nuts,
    chopped
1 10-oz can reduced-sodium
    and -fat cream of
    mushroom soup
1/2 cup chow mein noodles

Serves 3

Serving size:
1/3 recipe

1 Heat oven to 350°F. Combine all ingredients except chow mein noodles in a bowl.

2 Bake in a nonstick casserole dish (or spray a glass dish with nonstick cooking spray) for 30 minutes. Top with noodles to serve.

Exchanges
2 1/2 Starch
2 Lean Meat
1/2 Fat

Calories 321
  Calories from Fat . . 92
Total Fat . . . . 10 g
  Saturated Fat. . . . . . . 2 g
Cholesterol. . . . . 17 mg
Sodium. . . . . 700 mg
Carbohydrate . . . . . . 36 g
  Dietary Fiber . . . . 3 g
  Sugars . . . . 5 g
Protein . . . . 21 g

Vegetable Bake

1 1/2 cups mixed frozen
    vegetables, thawed
2 Tbsp flour
1 Tbsp margarine
1/4 cup fat-free milk
1 Tbsp Parmesan cheese
1 cup cooked mashed
    potatoes
Dash paprika

Serves 2

Serving size:
1/2 recipe

1 Heat oven to 350°F. Mix vegetables and flour in a small nonstick casserole dish (or spray a glass dish with nonstick cooking spray).

2 Melt margarine in a small saucepan and add milk and cheese. Pour hot liquid over vegetables. Top with mashed potatoes, spreading evenly. Sprinkle with paprika.

3 Bake 25–30 minutes or until potatoes slightly brown.

Exchanges
1 1/2 Starch
1 1/2 Fat

Calories 186
  Calories from Fat . . 67
Total Fat . . . . 7 g
  Saturated Fat. . . . . . . 2 g
Cholesterol. . . . . 4 mg
Sodium. . . . . 173 mg
Carbohydrate . . . . . . 26 g
  Dietary Fiber . . . . 3 g
  Sugars . . . . 5 g
Protein . . . . 6 g

Homemade Egg Substitute

3 egg whites
2 Tbsp fat-free dry milk
    powder
1 tsp fat-free milk
2–3 drops yellow food
    coloring

Serves 2

Serving size:
1/2 recipe

1 Mix ingredients in bowl with wire whisk. Use to substitute for 2 whole eggs.

Exchanges
1 Very Lean Meat

Calories 42
  Calories from Fat . . . 0
Total Fat . . . . 0 g
  Saturated Fat. . . . . . 0 g
Cholesterol. . . . . 1 mg
Sodium. . . . . 107 mg
Carbohydrate . . . . . . 3 g
  Dietary Fiber . . . . . . 0 g
  Sugars . . . . 3 g
Protein . . . . 7 g

Brown Rice Cups

1 cup cooked brown rice
1 tsp margarine, melted
1/4 cup shredded low-fat
    cheddar cheese
2 Tbsp fat-free milk
2 Tbsp dry breadcrumbs
Dash paprika

Serves 2

Serving size:
1/2 recipe

1 Heat oven to 350°F. Spray 2 glass custard cups (or use muffin tin) with nonstick cooking spray.

2 In a small bowl, combine all ingredients except paprika, mixing well. Spoon evenly into cups and press firmly to flatten tops. Sprinkle with paprika.

3 Bake 18–20 minutes or until light brown.

Exchanges
2 Starch
1 Fat

Calories 201
  Calories from Fat . . 56
Total Fat . . . . 6 g
  Saturated Fat . . . . . . 2 g
Cholesterol . . . . 10 mg
Sodium . . . . 207 mg
Carbohydrate . . . . . . 28 g
  Dietary Fiber . . . . 2 g
  Sugars . . . . 2 g
Protein . . . . 8 g

Pea and Carrot Salad

1 10-oz pkg frozen peas and
   carrots blend, cooked
1 hard-boiled egg, yolk
   removed
1 tsp dehydrated minced
   onion
 1/2 tsp celery seed
1/4 cup fat-free French or
   Ranch dressing
1 Tbsp chopped pimiento
   (optional)

Serves 4

Serving size:
1/4 recipe

1 Toss all ingredients, cover, and chill before serving.

Exchanges
1 Starch

Calories 78
  Calories from Fat . . . 3
Total Fat . . . . 0 g
  Saturated Fat. . . . . . . 0 g
Cholesterol. . . . . 0 mg
Sodium. . . . . 230 mg
Carbohydrate . . . . . . 13 g
  Dietary Fiber . . . . 3 g
  Sugars . . . . 5 g
Protein . . . . 4 g

Apple Raisin Crunch Salad

2 tart apples, cut into
    chunks
2 Tbsp raisins
1/4 cup Grapenuts(tm)
    cereal or wheat germ
1 cup fat-free lemon-flavored
    yogurt
4 lettuce leaves

Serves 4

Serving size:
1/4 recipe

1 Combine apple chunks, raisins, cereal, and yogurt in small bowl. Mix well. Spoon on lettuce leaves.

Exchanges
2 Carbohydrate

Calories	122
Calories from Fat	3
Total Fat	0 g
Saturated Fat	0 g
Cholesterol	1 mg
Sodium	87 mg
Carbohydrate	28 g
Dietary Fiber	3 g
Sugars	19 g
Protein	4 g

Rice Salad

1 cup cooked brown rice
1/2 cup chopped celery
2 Tbsp dried fruit
2 Tbsp dry roasted soy nuts
    or other nut
1 Tbsp olive oil
1 Tbsp lemon juice
1 11-oz can water- or juice-
    packed mandarin
    oranges, drained
1/4 cup chopped parsley

Serves 4

Serving size:
1/4 recipe

1 Combine all ingredients and stir well.

Exchanges
1 Starch
1/2 Fruit
1/2 Fat

Calories 137
  Calories from Fat . . 40
Total Fat . . . . 4 g
  Saturated Fat. . . . . . 1 g
Cholesterol . . . . 0 mg
Sodium . . . . 50 mg
Carbohydrate . . . . . . 21 g
  Dietary Fiber . . . . . . 3 g
  Sugars . . . . 7 g
Protein . . . . 4 g

Tropical Cooler

1 cup unsweetened
   pineapple juice
1 ripe banana, peeled and
   sliced
1 cup plain fat-free yogurt
1 Tbsp coconut
1/8 tsp nutmeg

Serves 2

Serving size:
1/2 recipe

1 Combine ingredients in blender and puree. Chill well before serving.

Exchanges
2 Fruit
1 Fat-Free Milk

Calories 196
   Calories from Fat . . 10
Total Fat . . . . 1 g
   Saturated Fat. . . . . . . 1 g
Cholesterol. . . . . 3 mg
Sodium. . . . . 103 mg
Carbohydrate . . . . . . 41 g
   Dietary Fiber . . . . 2 g
   Sugars . . . . 35 g
Protein . . . . 8 g

Spicy Baked Bean Soup

1 15-oz can navy or kidney
    beans, rinsed and
    drained
1 8-oz can sodium-free
    tomato sauce
4 oz water
1/4 tsp ground red pepper
3 Tbsp Barbecue Sauce
    (see recipe, page 57)
Dash hot pepper sauce

Serves 2

Serving size:
1/2 recipe

1 Combine ingredients in blender
and puree. Heat thoroughly and
serve with baked tortilla chips if
desired.

Exchanges
2 1/2 Starch
1 Very Lean Meat

Calories 223
  Calories from Fat . . . 7
Total Fat . . . . 1 g
  Saturated Fat. . . . . . . 0 g
Cholesterol. . . . . 0 mg
Sodium. . . . . 274 mg
Carbohydrate . . . . . . 41 g
  Dietary Fiber . . . . . . 10 g
  Sugars . . . . 11 g
Protein . . . . 14 g

High-Calcium Choices

Roman Burgers

1/2 lb lean ground beef
1/4 cup bread crumbs
1 tsp Italian seasoning
1/2 tsp garlic powder
2 Tbsp fat-free milk
1 Tbsp grated Parmesan
    cheese
2 Tbsp nonfat dry milk
    powder
2 Tbsp low-fat shredded
    mozzarella cheese

Serves 2

Serving size:
1 burger

1 Combine all ingredients except mozzarella cheese in a mixing bowl and form into two patties. Cook on grill or in skillet, turning once, until center is cooked through.

2 Sprinkle 1 Tbsp mozzarella cheese on top of each patty while still in pan and remove when cheese melts.

Exchanges
1 Starch
3 Lean Meat
1 1/2 Fat

Calories 327
  Calories from Fat . 161
Total Fat . . . . 18 g
  Saturated Fat . . . . . . 7 g
Cholesterol . . . . 80 mg
Sodium . . . . 306 mg
Carbohydrate . . . . . . 13 g
  Dietary Fiber . . . . 0 g
  Sugars . . . . 4 g
Protein . . . . 27 g

Popeye's Spinach Pie

1 9-inch pie shell
1 10-oz pkg frozen spinach,
    thawed and drained
1/4 cup frozen diced onion or
    pearl onions, thawed
2 Tbsp flour
1 Tbsp margarine, melted
1/2 cup egg substitute or 3
    egg whites
1/2 cup fat-free milk
2 Tbsp fat-free dry milk
    powder
1/2 cup low-fat cheese

Serves 6

Serving size:
1 piece

1 Heat oven to 425°F. Bake pie shell for 5–8 minutes. Reduce heat to 350°F.

2 Combine remaining ingredients in a bowl and spoon into pie shell. Bake 30–35 minutes or until center is puffed and lightly browned and a knife inserted in the center comes out clean.

Exchanges
1 Starch
1 Vegetable
2 Fat

Calories 186
  Calories from Fat . . 86
Total Fat . . . . 10 g
  Saturated Fat. . . . . . 3 g
Cholesterol. . . . . 3 mg
Sodium . . . . 304 mg
Carbohydrate . . . . . . 17 g
  Dietary Fiber . . . . . . 2 g
  Sugars . . . . 2 g
Protein . . . . 8 g

Fortified Milk

8 oz fat-free milk
2 Tbsp nonfat dry milk
    powder
1/4 tsp vanilla (optional)

Serves 1

Serving size:
1 cup

1 Combine ingredients and stir well. This is also a great way to "thicken" fat-free milk if you are changing from whole milk.

Exchanges
1 1/2 Fat-Free Milk

Calories 116
  Calories from Fat . . . 4
Total Fat . . . . 0 g
  Saturated Fat. . . . . . . 0 g
Cholesterol. . . . . 6 mg
Sodium. . . . . 173 mg
Carbohydrate . . . . . . 16 g
  Dietary Fiber . . . . 0 g
  Sugars . . . . 15 g
Protein . . . . 11 g

Calcium-Packed Pudding

1 1.4-oz pkg sugar-free
    instant pudding mix, any
    flavor
2 Tbsp fat-free dry milk
    powder
2 cups fat-free milk

Serves 2

Serving size:
1/2 recipe

1 Whisk ingredients for 2 minutes. Pour into desired containers and chill.

Exchanges
1 Carbohydrate
1 Fat-Free Milk

Calories 151
   Calories from Fat . . . 4
Total Fat . . . . 0 g
   Saturated Fat . . . . 0 g
Cholesterol . . . . 5 mg
Sodium . . . . 810 mg
Carbohydrate . . . . . . 26 g
   Dietary Fiber . . . . 0 g
   Sugars . . . . 13 g
Protein . . . . 10 g

Salmon Loaf

1 7.5-oz can salmon with
     bones
1 whole egg
1 egg white
2 Tbsp chopped green onions
1/4 tsp dried dill
1/4 cup fresh bread crumbs
     or low-sodium cracker
     crumbs
2 Tbsp fat-free dry milk
     powder
2 Tbsp fat-free milk
2 slices fat-free cheese, cut
     into four pieces

Serves 2

Serving size:
2 mini-loaves

1 Heat oven to 350°F. Combine all ingredients except the cheese in a medium bowl.

2 Spoon the batter into 4 nonstick muffin cups, filling 3/4 full. Top each with 2 pieces of cheese and bake 15–20 minutes.

Exchanges
1/2 Carbohydrate
4 Lean Meat

Calories 257
  Calories from Fat . . 82
Total Fat . . . . 9 g
  Saturated Fat. . . . . . . 1 g
Cholesterol . . . . . . 168 mg
Sodium . . . . 998 mg
Carbohydrate . . . . 9 g
  Dietary Fiber . . . . 0 g
  Sugars . . . . 6 g
Protein . . . . 33 g

Cows in the Orchard Salad

1/2 cup low-fat cottage
    cheese, small curd
1 15-oz can unsweetened
    mixed canned fruit,
    drained
1 Tbsp crushed nuts
2 lettuce leaves

Serves 2

Serving size:
1/2 recipe

1 Mix cottage cheese, fruit, and nuts in a bowl. Spoon onto lettuce leaves.

Exchanges
1 Very Lean Meat
1 1/2 Fruit

Calories	136
Calories from Fat	. . 26
Total Fat	3 g
Saturated Fat	1 g
Cholesterol	3 mg
Sodium	244 mg
Carbohydrate	21 g
Dietary Fiber	2 g
Sugars	19 g
Protein	8 g

Smashed Potatoes

2 medium boiled potatoes
1/2 cup fat-free milk
1 Tbsp margarine
1/4 tsp onion powder
2 Tbsp fat-free dry milk
    powder
1/4 cup shredded fat-free
    cheese
1/4 tsp salt

Serves 2

Serving size:
1/2 recipe

1 Whip all ingredients until smooth.

Exchanges
2 1/2 Starch
1/2 Fat-Free Milk
1/2 Fat

Calories 252
  Calories from Fat . . 54
Total Fat . . . . 6 g
  Saturated Fat. . . . . . 1 g
Cholesterol. . . . . 2 mg
Sodium. . . . . 321 mg
Carbohydrate . . . . . . 41 g
  Dietary Fiber . . . . . . 3 g
  Sugars . . . . 9 g
Protein . . . . 10 g

Berry Frappe

1/2 cup fresh berries
1 Tbsp sugar
1 cup fat-free milk
2 Tbsp nonfat dry milk
    powder
5 ice cubes

Serves 1

Serving size:
1 recipe

---

1 Blend all ingredients until frothy.

Exchanges
1 1/2 Carbohydrate
1 Fat-Free Milk

Calories 194
  Calories from Fat . . . 7
Total Fat . . . . 1 g
  Saturated Fat . . . . 0 g
Cholesterol . . . . 6 mg
Sodium . . . . 176 mg
Carbohydrate . . . . . . 36 g
  Dietary Fiber . . . . 2 g
  Sugars . . . . 32 g
Protein . . . . 12 g

Cheese Grits

1 cup cooked grits
2 Tbsp fat-free dry milk
    powder
2 Tbsp fat-free cheese,
    shredded
Dash garlic powder
    (optional)

Serves 1

Serving size:
1 cup

1 Mix well.

Exchanges
2 1/2 Starch

Calories 195
  Calories from Fat . . . 4
Total Fat . . . . 0 g
  Saturated Fat. . . . . . . 0 g
Cholesterol. . . . . 2 mg
Sodium. . . . . 239 mg
Carbohydrate . . . . . . 38 g
  Dietary Fiber . . . . 0 g
  Sugars . . . . 7 g
Protein . . . . 9 g

Creamy Carrot and Apple Salad

1 cup low-fat cottage cheese
1 Tbsp plus 1 tsp
   unsweetened fruit juice
1/2 cup shredded carrots
1 tart apple, diced
   (skin left on)
2 lettuce leaves

Serves 2

Serving size:
1/2 recipe

1 Blend cottage cheese and fruit juice until smooth.

2 Combine with carrots and apple. Spoon mixture on lettuce leaves to serve.

Exchanges
2 Very Lean Meat
1 Vegetable
1 Fruit

Calories 147
  Calories from Fat . . 14
Total Fat . . . . 2 g
  Saturated Fat. . . . . . 0 g
Cholesterol. . . . . 5 mg
Sodium. . . . . 450 mg
Carbohydrate . . . . . . 21 g
  Dietary Fiber . . . . . . 3 g
  Sugars . . . . 17 g
Protein . . . . 15 g

Simply Great Desserts

Classic Cherry Cola Gelatin

.3-oz pkg sugar-free cherry
    gelatin
1 cup hot water
1 cup diet cola (chilled)
1 15-oz can unsweetened
    cherries, drained
    (1 3/4 cups)
Fat-free non-dairy whipped
    topping (optional)

Serves 6

Serving size:
1/4 recipe

1 Dissolve gelatin in the hot water
and stir 2 minutes. Add cola and
cherries and stir.

2 Pour into desired mold. Chill
until firm. Top with whipped
topping, if desired.

Exchanges
1 Fruit

Calories 53
    Calories from Fat . . . 0
Total Fat . . . . 0 g
    Saturated Fat. . . . . . . 0 g
Cholesterol. . . . . 0 mg
Sodium. . . . . 45 mg
Carbohydrate . . . . . . 12 g
    Dietary Fiber . . . . 1 g
    Sugars . . . . 10 g
Protein . . . . 2 g

Skins-On Applesauce

6 medium-size tart apples,
   washed, seeds removed,
   and cut into chunks
1/4 cup sugar
1/2 tsp cinnamon

Serves 6

Serving size:
1/6 recipe

1 Heat oven to 350°F. Place apples evenly in a nonstick baking pan (or use a glass dish sprayed with nonstick cooking spray) and add enough water to half cover apples.

2 Mix the sugar and cinnamon together in a small bowl and sprinkle over apples. Cover with lid or aluminum foil. Bake approximately 1 1/4 hours or until apples are completely soft.

3 Carefully pour mixture in bowl. Mash with fork until desired consistency. Cool before serving.

Exchanges
2 Fruit

Calories 125
   Calories from Fat . . . 5
Total Fat . . . . 1 g
   Saturated Fat . . . . 0 g
Cholesterol . . . . 0 mg
Sodium . . . . 0 mg
Carbohydrate . . . . . . 32 g
   Dietary Fiber . . . . 4 g
   Sugars . . . . 28 g
Protein . . . . 0 g

Baked Peaches

4 canned peach halves
  (packed in own juice or
  water)
1 Tbsp brown sugar
1 tsp lemon juice
1/4 tsp ground nutmeg
2 graham cracker squares
2 Tbsp fat-free nondairy
  whipped topping

Serves 2

Serving size:
1/2 recipe

1 Heat oven to 350°F. Drain peach halves and place in 8 × 8-inch nonstick baking dish (or use a glass dish sprayed with nonstick cooking spray).

2 Sprinkle with sugar, lemon juice, and nutmeg. Bake 15–20 minutes.

3 Place each graham cracker square on a dessert plate. Top with 2 peach halves and 1 Tbsp whipped topping. Serve warm.

Exchanges
2 Carbohydrate

Calories 128
  Calories from Fat . . . 6
Total Fat . . . . 1 g
  Saturated Fat . . . . . . 0 g
Cholesterol . . . . 0 mg
Sodium . . . . 54 mg
Carbohydrate . . . . . . 30 g
  Dietary Fiber . . . . . . 2 g
  Sugars . . . . 24 g
Protein . . . . 1 g

New Brownies

4 egg whites
1/4 tsp salt
1 cup sugar
1 tsp vanilla
1 cup chocolate wafer cookie
    crumbs
1/2 cup chopped walnuts

Serves 8

Serving size:
1 brownie

1 Heat oven to 350°F. In a medium bowl, beat egg whites and salt with rotary mixer or wire whisk until soft peaks form. Slowly add sugar until peaks are glossy. Beat in vanilla.

2 Fold in cookie crumbs and walnuts. Pour mixture into a nonstick pie pan and carefully level mixture with spatula. Bake 30 minutes.

Exchanges
2 1/2 Carbohydrate
1 Fat

Calories 209
    Calories from Fat . . 59
Total Fat . . . . 7 g
    Saturated Fat . . . . . . 1 g
Cholesterol . . . . 0 mg
Sodium . . . . 182 mg
Carbohydrate . . . . . . 36 g
    Dietary Fiber . . . . . . 1 g
    Sugars . . . . 30 g
Protein . . . . 4 g

Strawberry Cloud Pie

1 1/2 cup sliced strawberries
8 oz lite cream cheese,
    softened
1/4 cup sugar
2–3 drops almond extract
2–3 drops red food coloring
1 cup fat-free nondairy
    whipped topping
1 ready-to-use reduced-fat
    graham cracker pie crust

Serves 6

Serving size:
1 piece

1 Layer 3/4 cup strawberries on bottom of crust. Mix cream cheese, sugar, and almond extract together.

2 Add food coloring and whipped topping 1 tablespoon at a time to the cream cheese mixture, using an electric mixer or stirring by hand.

3 Spoon filling over berries, spreading evenly. Chill at least 6 hours. Top with remaining berries to serve.

Exchanges
3 Carbohydrate
2 1/2 Fat

Calories	331
Calories from Fat	109
Total Fat	12 g
Saturated Fat	7 g
Cholesterol	27 mg
Sodium	307 mg
Carbohydrate	46 g
Dietary Fiber	1 g
Sugars	24 g
Protein	6 g

Sweet Bread Anytime

1/4 cup unsweetened fruit
    juice
2 tsp sugar
1 tsp cornstarch
1/2 cup sliced fresh fruit or
    unsweetened canned
    fruit
1 piece bread

Serves 1

Serving size:
1 recipe

1 Combine sugar and cornstarch. In a small saucepan, warm juice over medium heat.

2 Add sugar and cornstarch mixture to juice, stirring constantly until slightly thickened. Cool slightly.

3 Place the bread on a small plate and top with fruit. Pour sauce over top and let stand 1 minute.

Exchanges
2 1/2 Carbohydrate

Calories 176
  Calories from Fat . . 10
Total Fat . . . . 1 g
  Saturated Fat. . . . . . . 0 g
Cholesterol. . . . . 0 mg
Sodium. . . . . 140 mg
Carbohydrate . . . . . . 40 g
  Dietary Fiber . . . . 2 g
  Sugars . . . . 24 g
Protein . . . . 3 g

Chocolate Cookies

2 egg whites, beaten until
    stiff
2 tsp margarine, softened
1/2 cup sugar
1/2 cup flour
2 Tbsp cocoa powder
1/2 tsp vanilla
1/2 tsp baking powder
1/8 tsp salt

Serves 12

Serving size:
1 cookie

1 Heat oven to 350°F. Mix all ingredients in a small bowl.

2 Drop dough by spoonfuls on nonstick baking sheet. Bake 8–10 minutes.

Exchanges
1 Carbohydrate

Calories 65
   Calories from Fat . . . 7
Total Fat . . . . 1 g
   Saturated Fat. . . . . . . 0 g
Cholesterol. . . . . 0 mg
Sodium . . . . 57 mg
Carbohydrate . . . . . . 14 g
   Dietary Fiber . . . . 0 g
   Sugars . . . . 8 g
Protein . . . . 1 g

Kool Kabob

2 extra-large strawberries,
    cut in half
1/2 medium banana, sliced
    into 1-inch pieces
8 seedless grapes, washed

Serves 1

Serving size:
1 kabob

1 Place the fruit on a skewer,
alternating pieces. Place in
freezer for 1 hour.

2 Let stand in room temperature
5 minutes before eating.

Exchanges
1 1/2 Fruit

Calories 98
  Calories from Fat . . . 6
Total Fat . . . . 1 g
  Saturated Fat . . . . . . 0 g
Cholesterol . . . . 0 mg
Sodium . . . . 2 mg
Carbohydrate . . . . . . 25 g
  Dietary Fiber . . . . . . 3 g
  Sugars . . . . 17 g
Protein . . . . 1 g

Apricot Candy

2 oz bittersweet chocolate
1/4 tsp vanilla
6 dried apricot halves

1 Put chocolate and vanilla in a small oven-safe glass bowl or cup. Place in small skillet filled half full with water to create a small double-boiler. Melt chocolate over low heat.

2 With a toothpick, pick up apricot halves, dip into chocolate, and place on waxed paper to cool. Refrigerate to store.

Exchanges
1 Carbohydrate
1 1/2 Fat

Calories 111
  Calories from Fat . . 73
Total Fat . . . . 8 g
  Saturated Fat. . . . . . 4 g
Cholesterol . . . . 0 mg
Sodium . . . . 1 mg
Carbohydrate . . . . . . 14 g
  Dietary Fiber . . . . 2 g
  Sugars . . . . 9 g
Protein . . . . 2 g

Individual Blackberry Mini-Cakes

1/2 cup flour
1/4 cup sugar
1 Tbsp canola oil
1/4 cup fat-free milk
1/2 tsp baking powder
1/4 tsp salt
1/4 tsp vanilla
1 egg white
2 Tbsp reduced-sugar
    blackberry jam
3 Tbsp fat-free nondairy
    whipped topping

Serves 3

Serving size:
1 mini-cake

1 Heat oven to 350°F. Spray 3 6-oz custard cups with nonstick cooking spray.

2 In a small bowl, mix all ingredients except jam. Spoon batter equally into custard cups.

3 Add jam to center of each cup. Bake 12–15 minutes or until lightly browned on top. Cool. Top each cake 1 Tbsp whipped topping to serve.

Exchanges
2 1/2 Carbohydrate
1 Fat

Calories 217
  Calories from Fat . . 44
Total Fat . . . . 5 g
  Saturated Fat. . . . . . . 0 g
Cholesterol. . . . . 0 mg
Sodium. . . . . 290 mg
Carbohydrate . . . . . . 39 g
  Dietary Fiber . . . . 1 g
  Sugars . . . . 20 g
Protein . . . . 4 g

Resources

Sample Weekly Menu

Day 1

MEAL	MENU IDEA
Breakfast	Hot Apple Oatmeal recipe (page 32) Toast Fat-free milk Coffee
Lunch	Cream of Broccoli Soup recipe (page 56) Peaches (packed in juice or water) Unsalted crackers Unsweetened apple juice
Dinner	Pasta Spicy Pasta Sauce recipe (page 59) Lettuce and vegetable salad Bread Berries
Dessert	Chocolate Cookies recipe (page 146) Fat-free milk

Day 2

MEAL	MENU IDEA
Breakfast	Low-Fat Granola recipe (page 40) Banana Fat-free milk Coffee
Lunch	Anytime Fruit Salad recipe (page 68) Cereal Muffins recipe (page 33) Carrot sticks
Dinner	Instant Picnic recipe (page 50) Bread Pineapple (packed in juice or water)
Dessert	Baked Peaches recipe (page 142)

Day 3

MEAL	MENU IDEA
Breakfast	Cereal Muffins recipe (page 33) Homemade Egg Substitute recipe (page 119) Orange juice Coffee
Lunch	Turkey Sandwich Dilly Cucumber recipe (page 84) Graham crackers Applesauce
Dinner	Power Burger recipe (page 65) Homemade Catsup recipe (page 63) Easy Baked Potato Bites recipe (page 58) Steamed broccoli Fat-free milk
Dessert	Kool Kabob recipe (page 147)

Day 4

MEAL	MENU IDEA
Breakfast	Cornflakes with berries Toast Fortified Milk recipe (page 130) Coffee
Lunch	Cereal Muffins recipe (page 33) Chef salad with sliced turkey, lettuce, peppers, onion, mushroom, and tomatoes Fat-free dressing Banana
Dinner	Baked Ham Steak recipe (page 70) Rice Cooked carrots Pineapple (packed in juice or water)
Dessert	Snicker Wafers recipe (page 49)

Day 5

MEAL	MENU IDEA
Breakfast	Berry Frappe recipe (page 135) Toast Coffee
Lunch	Cows in the Orchard Salad recipe (page 133) Turkey frank with salsa Bread Graham crackers
Dinner	Coleslaw Salad recipe (page 87) Veal Scallopini with Lemon Sauce recipe (page 81) Sautéed Mushrooms recipe (page 82) Pasta
Dessert	Strawberry Cloud Pie recipe (page 144)

Day 6

MEAL	MENU IDEA
Breakfast	Chocolate Pancakes recipe (page 38) Fat-free milk Mandarin oranges (packed in juice or water)
Lunch	Sloppy Joes recipe (page 75) Graham crackers Grapes Carrot sticks
Dinner	Cabbage Patch Casserole recipe (page 52) Bread Unsweetened applesauce
Dessert	Classic Cherry Cola Gelatin recipe (page 140)

Day 7

MEAL	MENU IDEA
Breakfast	Cheese Grits recipe (page 136) Homemade Egg Substitute recipe (page 119) Banana Coffee
Lunch	Turkey frank Bread Chilled Mixed Vegetable Salad recipe (page 74) Orange juice
Dinner	Oven-Fried Chicken Legs recipe (page 61) Braised Cabbage recipe (page 83) Unsweetened applesauce Bread
Dessert	New Brownies recipe (page 143)

Grocery List

Pantry Staples

Baking powder
Bread crumbs
Brown sugar
Canola oil
Cocoa
Coffee
Crackers
Diet cola
Flour
Honey
Low-sodium bouillon
Pepper
Salt
Spices: cinnamon, caraway seeds, thyme, nutmeg, basil, oregano, garlic powder, onion powder, dry mustard, red pepper, paprika, cloves, parsley, and dill
Sugar
Vanilla extract
Vinegar

Grocery List

Almonds
Apple juice
Applesauce (unsweetened)
Bananas
Berries
Bread
Broccoli
Cabbage
Canned corn
Canned cherries in juice or water
Canned Mandarin oranges in juice or water
Canned peaches in juice or water

Canned pineapple in juice or water
Carrots
Cilantro
Cooked small shrimp
Cooked whole chicken
Cornflakes cereal
Cucumber
Dehydrated minced onion
Diet gelatin (lemon or lime and cherry)
Eggs
Fat-free dry milk powder
Fat-free Italian and French dressings
Fat-free milk
Fat-free whipped nondairy topping
Graham crackers
Grapes
Lean ground beef or pork
Lean sliced turkey
Lettuce
Light cream cheese
Low-fat chocolate wafer cookies
Low-fat cottage cheese
Low-sodium tomato paste
Margarine
Mushrooms
Nuts (walnuts or pecans)
Oat bran
Oatmeal
Onion
Orange juice (unsweetened)
Pasta
Potatoes
Raisins
Ready-to-use low-fat graham cracker pie crust
Reduced-fat cream of potato soup
Reduced-fat turkey franks
Rice
Salsa
Veal slices
Wheat germ
Zucchini

Emergency Food Shelf

There will be times when you may not be able to go and get food items due to illness, transportation problems, or weather conditions. Because it is extremely important for someone with diabetes to maintain a regular meal schedule to prevent problems with blood glucose control, preparing an emergency food shelf may help avoid problems. The four issues to consider when preparing an emergency food shelf are location, storage containers, selection of food items, and regular inspections of the area.

Choose a dark, cool, dry location for your emergency food shelf. Food will spoil quicker if kept in direct sunlight, warm areas, or moist environments. A good place may be on the top shelf in your pantry, or top shelf in your hallway linen closet. Basement locations are also good choices, provided they are free from moisture.

Storage containers are very important. Do not use containers you have recycled from food products, such as empty margarine bowls or frozen food containers. Use storage containers designed for food storage only. They will be made of thicker plastic materials and have tighter-fitting lids to prevent contact with the outside environment. It is important to keep food tightly covered at all times not only to help prevent spoilage, but also to prevent insect invasion.

Try to keep items in their original factory-sealed package, but for extra protection, use another layer of plastic. Seal dry goods such as flours, sugars, cereals, crackers, and cookies in plastic food storage bags. These items, along with small foods such as dried fruit, packages of tea, cocoa, and other items may also be placed in screw-top glass food jars. You can wash out and rinse old plastic milk jugs for water storage. Place items in a cardboard box if you want to keep the dust out.

Having a good variety of food items available in your food emergency shelf will pay off on days you are ill or cannot get out to purchase foods. Here is a list of suggested food items to have on hand, along with suggestions for storage duration.

Suggested Foods

(indefinite storage)
Bouillon cubes
Dry pasta
Evaporated fat-free milk
Instant gelatins (regular and diet)
Instant puddings (regular and diet)
Instant tea, coffee, or cocoa
Rice
Salt

(use within one year)
Canned nuts
Canned salmon, tuna, and chicken
Canned soups
Canned unsweetened juice (small cans)
Canned vegetable juice (small cans)
Factory bottled water
Flour and cornmeal
Instant cereals (cold and hot)
Instant potatoes
Jelly and jam
Peanut butter
Powdered milk in cans
Single serving cans of fruit and vegetables
Vegetable oils

(use within six months)
Cookies
Crackers
Dried fruit
Granola bars or breakfast bars
Home bottled water

In case of emergencies when you may lose electricity or water, you may find the following items handy:
Baby wipes
Foil
Manual can opener

Matches
Napkins
Paper plates
Paper towels
Plastic cups
Plastic utensils
Saran wrap
Sterno can
Storage bags
Styrofoam cups

Inspections

Check your emergency food shelf at least once a season. Rotate food items to assure freshness. Check containers for leaks, rust, holes, or insect damage. Discard any item with damage and replace it. Clean containers, if needed, and repackage items. Update your food shelf with your own new ideas and current food preferences.

Being prepared may save you from being hungry in the future. If transportation to the grocery store is a problem and you find yourself dipping into your food emergency shelf often, consider a home meal delivery program or grocery delivery service. If you live alone, you may also want to make sure you have emergency phone numbers (for physicians, utility companies, family, and friends) written down in one place so you can access them quickly.

An emergency food shelf is a great idea, and so is having an emergency medical shelf with diabetes testing supplies and some standard home first aid supplies and medications. Talk to your physician, pharmacist, or health care professional about storage for your current medications. Find out which over-the-counter medications for common illnesses and sick days are acceptable in your treatment plan, and keep a small supply available for days you may need them. Keep a list of your medications written down in case of an emergency for ordering refills or communicating with health care professionals. There may be times when you have to use a different doctor or pharmacy in an emergency, and they may not have access to all your past information.

Available Nutrition Services

Meal Services/Food Procurement

- The Administration of Aging (AOA) has an Elderly Nutrition Program (ENP) that provides support for group meals and home-delivered meals. These services may be based out of senior citizen centers, schools, churches, and other community agencies. To find out about an ENP service in your area, call Eldercare Locator, 1-800-677-1116, or contact www.fns.usda.gov/fdd/MENU/APPLICANTS/ELDERLY/npeho
- Food stamp information can be obtained from your local social services agency, or by contacting: www.fns.usda.gov/fsp/.

Other Services to Try

- Food and Nutrition Information Center, (301) 504-5719
- Local (Private) and Government Meals On Wheels/Home Delivered Meal Services, (703) 548-5558, www.projectmeal.org/.
- Local American Red Cross
- Local health department
- Local hospital
- Local senior citizen's center
- Local social services agency
- National Association of Nutrition and Aging Service Programs, (616) 531-9909
- National Resource Center on Nutrition and Aging, (305) 348-1517

Nutrition Information Services

- American Diabetes Association, 1-800-DIABETES, or (703) 549-1500, www.diabetes.org
- American Heart Association, (214) 373-6300
- Calcium Information Center, (800) 321-2681
- Food Allergy Network, (800) 929-4040, www.foodallergy.org
- Food and Drug Administration, consumer food information hotline (202) 205-4314
- Food and Drug Administration, consumer information services (888) 463-6332, www.fda.gov/oca/oca.htm
- Food and Nutrition for Native Americans, Indian Health Services Diabetes Program, (505) 248-4182

- Food and Nutrition Information Center, USDA, (301) 504-5719, www.naic@aoa.gov or www.nalusda.gov. For Braille, large print, or audio versions of information, contact (202) 720-2600
- National Center for Chronic Disease Prevention and Health Promotion Division of Diabetes Translation, (877) 232-3422, www.cdc.gov/nccdphp/ddt
- National Center for Complementary and Alternative Medicine Clearinghouse, (888) 644-6226
- National Clearinghouse for Alcohol and Drug Information Specialist, (301) 468-2600, www.health.org
- National Council for Reliable Health Information, (816) 228-4595, www.ncahf.org
- National Diabetes Information Clearinghouse, (301) 654-3327, www.niddk.nih.gov
- The American Dietetic Association, (800) 366-1655, www.eatright.org

Magazines and Newsletters on Nutrition

- *Diabetes Forecast*, American Diabetes Association, 1-800-DIABETES
- *FDA Consumer*, FDA, HFI-40, Rockville, MD 20857
- *Mayo Clinic Health Letter*, (800) 333-9037
- *Tufts University Health Nutrition Letter*, (800) 274-7581

Books and Pamphlets

- American Association of Retired Persons, (800) 424-3410, www.aarp.org
- American Diabetes Association (many selections), 1-800-DIABETES, www.diabetes.org
- American Dietetic Association (many selections), (800) 877-1600, www.eatright.org (Free articles on seniors and nutrition include "Boning Up on Calcium," "Calcium in Your Life," "The New Cholesterol Countdown," "Seniors: Eat Well for Good Health," "Staying Healthy—A Guide for Older Adults," and more).
- American Heart Association (many selections), (214) 373-6300
- Consumer Information Center, (800) 878-3256

Services for Older Adults

SERVICE/AGENCY	DESCRIPTION	PHONE	WEBSITE
Access America for Seniors	Website location for links to services for seniors		www.seniors.gov/health/html
American Association of Retired Persons	Newsletters, magazines, information for seniors, health and life insurance plans, advocacy groups, resources of many topics of interest for seniors	1-800-424-3410	www.aarp.org
American Cancer Society	Cancer information, prevention, cancer treatment information, and research studies.	1-800-227-2345	www.cancer.org
American Diabetes Association	Information on diabetes, diabetes books, cookbooks, resources, access to diabetes advocacy groups, membership, preventive care information, books, magazines, newsletter, website information, research information, referral source for diabetes education services and much more	1-800-DIABETES	www.diabetes.org

American Heart Association	Information and resource materials regarding heart disease and stroke prevention	1-800-242-8721	www.americanheart.org
American Medical Association	Physician location and credentialing body; general health information	1-800-621-8335	www.ama-assn.org/
Arthritis Foundation	Information line on arthritis, current treatments	1-800-283-7800	www.arthritis.org
Consumer Information Center	Free and low-cost pamphlets and booklets on finance, nutrition, health, planning for emergencies, legal topics and other topics	1-888-8PUEBLO	www.pueblo.gas.gov/
Consumer Product Safety Commission	Obtain safety information on products	1-800-638-2722	
Food and Drug Administration	Consumer protection and information about foods and drugs	1-888-463-6332	www.fda.gov

Continued

SERVICE/AGENCY	DESCRIPTION	PHONE	WEBSITE
Local Cooperative Extension Service	Information on nutrition, family resources, cooking classes, hobby ideas, education classes, newsletters, and other services		
Local Council on Aging	Referral service for needs of older adults		
Local Health Department, Hospital, or Health Care Facility	Health care, health education, diabetes education, nutrition education, support groups, pharmacy services, flu shots, preventive care, and more		
Local Library	Books, magazines, free access to internet, computer searches, video lending libraries, books on tape		
Local Lion's Club	Assistance for preventative eye care, donated eye glasses		

Local Senior Citizens Center	Support groups, free group meals, exercise classes, activities, adult day care options, advocacy groups, resource centers, information on local agencies for specific disorders, education opportunities	
Local Social Services Office	Housing, food stamps, financial information, access to other services	
Medicare	Benefits and information	1-800-MEDICARE
National Aging Information Center	Resources on housing, legal issues, nutrition, food services, locator service for access to local agencies for older adults and much more	1-202-619-7501 www.aoa.dhhs.gov/naic
National Association for Hispanic Elderly	Services and information for Hispanic older adults	1-626-564-1988 www.anppm@aol.com

Continued

SERVICE/AGENCY	DESCRIPTION	PHONE	WEBSITE
National Center for Complementary and Alternative Medicine Clearinghouse	Complementary medicine treatments, herbal treatments, nutritional supplementation, holistic medicine, aromatherapy, and other alternative medicine treatments	1-888-644-6226	www.altmed.od.nih.gov/nccam
National Dairy Council	Information on nutrition, health promotion, and osteoporosis	1-800-426-8271	www.dairyinfo.com
National Institute on Aging	Information for older adults regarding health and social services, research studies, resource network	1-800-222-2225	www.nih.gov/nia
North American Menopause Society	Information for women regarding menopause and women's health issues	1-800-774-5343	www.menopause.org
Office of Minority Health Resource Center	Information, education, and health resources for minorities	1-800-444-6472	www.omhrc.gov

Osteoporosis and Related Bone Disease National Resource Center (NIH)	Information on osteoporosis, educational materials	1-800-624-BONE www.osteo.org
Social Security Administration	Social Security income, benefits	1-800-772-1213
State Department for the Blind	Services and resources for the blind, information on access to books on tape, and reading services	
Veteran Affairs	Benefits and services for veterans	1-800-827-1000

Equivalent Measures

MEASURE	EQUIVALENT MEASURE
3 tsp	1 Tbsp
16 Tbsp	1 cup
2 cups	1 pint, or 16 fluid ounces
4 cups	1 quart
4 Tbsp	1/4 cup
5 1/2 Tbsp	1/3 cup
5 ml	1 tsp
15 ml	1 Tbsp
50 ml	1/2 cup minus 2 tsp
500 ml	1 pint plus 2 Tbsp
1 liter	1 quart plus 1 Tbsp
28 grams	1 ounce
464 grams	1 pound
1 kg	2 pounds plus 3 1/2 ounces
1 inch	2.5 centimeters (cm)

Glossary of Nutrition Terms

WORD	DEFINITION
Calories	Units representing the amount of energy provided by food. Carbohydrate, protein, and fat are the primary sources of calories in the diet, but alcohol also provides calories. If all calories consumed aren't used as energy, they may be stored as fat.
Carbohydrate (1 gram = 4 calories)	One of the three major sources of calories in the diet. Carbohydrates are broken down into glucose during digestion and is the main nutrient that raises blood glucose levels. Food containing carbohydrates include sugars, jams, jellies, honey, breads, pastas, potatoes, corn, peas, grains, beans, fruits, fruit juices, vegetables, milk, and candies. The percentage of calories you get from carbohydrate must be determined with your health care team. It depends on your food preferences and the goals set for your blood glucose and lipid levels.
Carbohydrate Counting	A method of meal planning focusing on the amount of carbohydrate eaten to help blood glucose control. Carbohydrate foods cause the greatest rises in blood glucose compared to fat- and protein-containing foods. The method involves determining carbohydrate quantities in food and following prescribed amounts at meals and snacks.

WORD	DEFINITION
Cholesterol	A waxy, fat-like substance used by the body to build cell walls and make certain vitamins and hormones. The liver produces enough cholesterol for the body but we also get cholesterol from animal products. Eating too much saturated fat can cause the blood cholesterol to rise and collect along the inside walls of blood vessels. This increases risk of heart attack and stroke.

On average, consume less than 300 milligrams of cholesterol per day. |
Daily Value	A reference value for a nutrient based on 2200 calories used for nutrition label comparisons.
Exchanges	A food group system developed by the American Diabetes Association and the American Dietetic Association for meal planning. There are seven basic groups: Starch, Other Carbohydrates, Meat and Meat Substitutes, Vegetable, Fruit, Milk, and Fat. Any food in a given group can be exchanged for any other food in that group in the appropriate amount.
Fats **(1 gram = 9 calories)**	The most concentrated source of calories in the diet. There are two main types of fats, saturated and unsaturated. Saturated fats are found primarily in animal products. Unsaturated fats mainly come from plants, and can be monounsaturated (olive or canola oil, for example), or polyunsaturated (corn and other vegetable blend oils, for example). Excess intake of fat, especially saturated fat, can cause elevated blood cholesterol, increasing the risk of heart disease and stroke.

WORD	DEFINITION
	Work with your health care team to determine the right amount of fat for your meal plan. The amount will depend on your weight, your blood glucose and blood lipid goals, and your overall health. No more than 10 percent of the calories in your diet should come from saturated fats.
Fiber	The parts of plants that the body can't digest, such as fruit and vegetable skins and seeds. Fiber aids in the normal functioning of the digestive system, specifically the intestinal tract. Fiber is the only carbohydrate that does not raise blood glucose or provide calories. Consume 20–35 grams of fiber from a wide variety of food sources.
Free Foods	Foods with less than 20 calories per serving in the food exchange system.
Glucose	A simple form of sugar that acts as the body's fuel. It is produced when foods are broken down in the digestive system. Glucose is carried by the blood to cells. The amount of glucose in the blood is known as the blood glucose level.
Good Source of _____(nutrient)	A food that contains 10–19% of the Daily Value for a particular nutrient.
High Source of _____(nutrient)	A food that contains 20% or more of the Daily Value for a particular nutrient.

WORD	DEFINITION
Protein (1 gram = 4 calories)	One of the three major sources of calories in the diet. Protein provides the body with material for building blood cells, body tissue, hormones, and other important substances. It is found in meats, eggs, milk, and certain vegetables and starches. If you do not have signs of kidney disease, between 10–20% of calories should come from protein in the diet. If you develop kidney disease, a maximum protein intake of 0.8 gram of protein per kilogram of body weight per day is usually recommended. This is about 43 grams for a 120-pound person, 54 grams for a 150-pound person and 65 grams for a 180-pound person.
Sodium	A chemical that comprises 40% of salt, a necessary nutrient for the body. Many health authorities recommend limiting sodium intake to no more than 2,400 to 3,00 milligrams per day. For people with high blood pressure, check with your health care professional to determine your appropriate sodium intake.
Sugar	A form of carbohydrate that provides calories and raises blood glucose levels. There are a variety of sugars, such as white, brown, confectioners', invert, and raw. Fructose, lactose, sucrose, maltose, dextrose, glucose, honey, corn syrup, molasses, and sorghum are also sugars.

WORD	DEFINITION
	Sugar and sugar-containing items are allowed in a diabetes meal plan. However, these foods need to be balanced within the meal plan, and may need to be substituted for other carbohydrate-containing foods. Consult your RD to help you learn how to use sugar and sugar-containing foods within your meal plan.
Sugar Substitutes	Sweeteners used in place of sugar. Some sugar substitutes have calories and will affect blood glucose levels to some extent, such as fructose (a sugar, but often used in "sugar-free" products) and sugar alcohols like sorbitol and mannitol. Others have very few calories and will not affect blood glucose levels, such as saccharin, acesulfame-K, aspartame, and sucralose.

Alphabetical List of Recipes

Subject Index

About the American Diabetes Association

The American Diabetes Association is the nation's leading voluntary health organization supporting diabetes research, information, and advocacy. Its mission is to prevent and cure diabetes and to improve the lives of all people affected by diabetes. The American Diabetes Association is the leading publisher of comprehensive diabetes information. Its huge library of practical and authoritative books for people with diabetes covers every aspect of self-care—cooking and nutrition, fitness, weight control, medications, complications, emotional issues, and general self-care.

To order American Diabetes Association books: Call 1-800-232-6733. http://store.diabetes. org (Note: there is no need to use www when typing this particular Web address.)

To join the American Diabetes Association: Call 1-800-806-7801. www.diabetes.org/ membership

For more information about diabetes or ADA programs and services: Call 1-800-342-2383. E-mail: Customerservice@diabetes.org

To locate an ADA/NCQA Recognized Provider of quality diabetes care in your area: Call 1-703-549-1500 ext. 2202. www.diabetes.org/recognition/Physicians/ListAll.asp

To find an ADA Recognized Education Program in your area: Call 1-888-232-0822. www.diabetes.org/recognition/education.asp

To join the fight to increase funding for diabetes research, end discrimination, and improve insurance coverage: Call 1-800-342-2383. www.diabetes.org/advocacy

To find out how you can get involved with the programs in your community: Call 1-800-342-2383. See below for program Web addresses.

- American Diabetes Month: Educational activities aimed at those diagnosed with diabetes—month of November. www.diabetes.org/ADM
- American Diabetes Alert: Annual public awareness campaign to find the undiagnosed—held the fourth Tuesday in March. www.diabetes.org/alert
- The Diabetes Assistance & Resources Program (DAR): diabetes awareness program targeted to the Latino community. www.diabetes.org/DAR
- African American Program: diabetes awareness program targeted to the African American community. www.diabetes.org/africanamerican
- Awakening the Spirit: Pathways to Diabetes Prevention & Control: diabetes awareness program targeted to the Native American community. www.diabetes.org/ awakening

To find out about an important research project regarding type 2 diabetes: www. diabetes.org/ada/research.asp

To obtain information on making a planned gift or charitable bequest: Call 1-888-700-7029. www.diabetes.org/ada/plan.asp

To make a donation or memorial contribution: Call 1-800-342-2383. www.diabetes. org/ada/cont.asp